IT'S NOT
ABOUT THE
MANGOS

Organizational Success Means
PUTTING PEOPLE FIRST

IT'S NOT
ABOUT THE
MANGOS

Organizational Success Means
PUTTING PEOPLE FIRST

Kent Coleman

Cover design by Miblart
Interior print design and layout by Sydnee Hyer
Ebook design and layout by Sydnee Hyer

Published by TireGuyPress

Paperback ISBN: 978-0-578-34568-0
Hardcover ISBN: 978-0-578-28220-6

Please sign up for my newsletter at www.kentcoleman.com and find links to my social media, @TireGuyKent. I love to hear from my readers.

*"I think I have learned that the best way to lift one's self up
is to help some one else."*

—Booker T. Washington

Contents

Introduction

It's Not About the Mangos

"The most beautiful stories always start with wreckage."
—Jack London

In 2008, two years after buying one of the highest revenue-producing tire stores in the nation, our sales began spiraling downward—quickly. At age 28, I knew nothing about the automotive world. I literally did not know the difference between a tire and a wheel. In 2006, when my brother and I bought the crowded little five-bay Big O Tires store in downtown Salt Lake City, it was bringing in $6 million in sales. Typical shops of that size had an annual revenue of around $1 million, maybe $2 million. But as the economic recession roared, sales in 2008 plummeted to $4.9 million at my shop. All I could think of to save the business was to lay off some of our most expensive employees. That decision nearly bankrupted me as sales continued falling to $4.1 million in 2009 and I depended heavily on store revenue to make our big loan payments.

In the elevator, right after the national Big O Tires awards banquet for our franchise chain in Dallas, a guy I did not know looked at my name tag and asked, "Are you with the 9th South store in Salt Lake City?"

I replied, "Yes."

Looking puzzled, he asked, "That store was legendary. Didn't it used to be number one in the country?"

I got off the elevator without answering.

A Rough Start

Those who know me personally, and especially those in the tire franchise business, may find it hard to believe that conversation on the elevator back in 2010 ever took place. We've come a long way since then, to be sure. But the early days were rough. That was largely due to my ignorance back then about the important role people play in creating a company culture that generates a successful environment in which everyone—owners, operators, managers, and employees—can not only survive but can become great.

How I got started in the tire business, which ultimately landed me in that elevator with a fellow franchise owner asking me questions for which I had no answers, was purely by chance. In the spring of 2006, my brother Kory met a guy who was selling a Big O Tires auto repair franchise. Kory had more home equity than I did, and he knew I was on the hunt for a new project after selling the small scrapbooking company my sister and I had founded. So when the opportunity came up to purchase a successful retail store, he and I borrowed the money to buy a franchise in Murray, Utah. I was excited and confident, but I did not yet understand what it meant to try to lead a team. Although Kory was my business partner, he was working full-time managing a multi-state division of a large corporation. He provided financial backing and great advice but was not involved in the day-to-day.

Despite jumping in mostly alone, I was enthusiastic. Entrepreneurship was in my blood, and the thought of what we could accomplish, while nerve-racking, was exhilarating as well. My computer was full of spreadsheets detailing our future success. My daydreams were full of nice vacations. But those visions of grandeur were just numbers on a screen; they weren't real life. They existed only in my own head. I did not yet see the role that other people would need to play for those dreams to have a shot at becoming reality.

Within a few months, we bought another Big O Tires store in Salt Lake City, known as the "9th South" location, which just happened to be the number one revenue franchise of that chain in the country, out of about 500 stores. We secured a large loan to purchase that shop in December of 2006, when credit was easy to get. We should not have been able to obtain that loan, and no bank in their right mind would ever give it to us today under those same circumstances. Before we knew it, we had a couple of tire stores doing a total of $9 million in revenue, we had almost no working capital, and my co-workers will attest that I knew absolutely nothing about tires, car repair, or running a multi-million-dollar franchise. Oh, and the global financial crisis was about to begin the next year.

Our fairly precarious financial situation and my lack of major team-building experience were perfect complements to my dearth of knowledge and experience in the auto service industry. It began to dawn on me the trouble I might be in when I attended a three-week training course in Denver, a requirement for getting the franchise. Of the six new students, I was the only one without auto shop experience . . . and that was obvious within about five minutes. The other students and the instructors were shocked that I did not know a thing about the business.

The first week of instruction covered all things tire-related. The language was completely new to me—I knew nothing about tire sizes, speed ratings, or siping; nothing about plies, LT versus passenger, HP, or UHP. My pen burned holes in my notebook as I struggled to write down what teachers said would be the difference between making money and going out of business.

After explaining how to sell a tire, the instructor made each of us take a turn in front of the class, selling a tire. I watched and listened in a sort of quiet terror, hoping for the lunch break so everyone would forget about me. As the others showed their knowledge with a litany of tire features and benefits, I thought, *I have bought tires, but never once have I known or cared about siping, speed ratings, or rubber compounds. I don't think I need to know this stuff in order to sell tires.*

Unfortunately, we didn't break for lunch, they didn't forget about me, and my turn came up. Instead of focusing on technical details about a tire, which I didn't feel a potential customer would ever be concerned with, I sold the tire with the simple points I cared about, and I made that sales pitch using words I understood. I said, "This is my favorite tire. It is safe, it has a 60,000-mile warranty, and it is worth its price. I am very confident you'll love it."

Of course, this wasn't what the teacher wanted to hear. He said, "Kent, you need to tell us at least three other features of the tire. Do you need to look at your notes?"

I replied, "I know the features, but I get bored thinking about them. The vast majority of regular people couldn't care less about those features. More information is just clutter—it will create confusion and uncertainty about having to pick the *correct* tire from a wall full of 16 different options. Most people want confidence and simplicity." Then

I sat down as the egotistical rookie who thought he knew better than a room of veterans.

The instructor looked at me, shook his head, and said, "You'll see." The next week we were taught about "service." This included oil changes and all kinds of repairs. The teacher went into great detail about brake types, and the terms he used were vaguely familiar to me. It had never crossed my mind to care what these terms meant. As the other students nodded with boredom due to the elementary level of the subject matter, I got a knot in my stomach, and beads of sweat formed on my forehead. Even with the instructor's explanations and my feverish note-taking, I still didn't get it; it was over my head. (My brain rebels against trying to understand all things mechanical, as ironic as that may be for a tire store owner!)

We then divided into pairs to practice explaining brake systems to another student in the class. I asked my partner to go first, hoping that would help me get more prepared. It didn't help. I was beyond help when it came to anything automotive. After thinking I was pretty cool for my take on selling tires, I knew right away that my ability to talk about brakes was going to be ugly. My attempt was feeble, and the instructor was right there, listening to me and staring at me intently. The other students in the room were also staring at me before they slowly looked down into nothing in their laps.

At that moment, I was all alone on an island. The other students were great guys, very nice, but they were the same in one regard while I was different. They easily understood these concepts, and I did not. But I was not concerned about being all alone in this—at the time, anyway. My problem going forward, however, became this "alone-ness," where I failed to see the value in others and felt that I had to figure everything out on my own.

When I finished my nonsensical rambling about brakes, the instructor said, "Kent, I am very worried about you. I am not going to be able to recommend you for a franchise."

The Experiment Begins

The teacher was right to be worried: I was indeed clueless. Despite all of this, my brother and I did manage to get the top-producing 9th South store in Salt Lake City. The employees seemed shocked that a 28-year-old with no automotive knowledge or experience had become the new owner. Most of the crew members were seasoned, skilled veterans who knew how to make sales happen. Within a few weeks, the top salesperson at the store was recruited by another location and quit because he didn't like how things were going. Some of our employees actually told customers and vendors that I wouldn't last two years before going out of business. In no time, the 9th South location went from an exciting place to one of pessimism and doubt. The crew was skeptical and unimpressed, and sales started to decline. Customers were still coming in, but morale was down and I was not sure how to rally the team.

It was obvious that the negative energy among the crew hurt sales, even though it was hard to quantify its effects. As the 2008 financial recession set in over the next year or two, sales continued to spiral downward. In 2008, at the beginning of the crisis, we were down 18 percent from the store's 2006 high, and by 2009 we had lost over 30 percent of revenue. Kory and I had obtained large loans to buy the franchises, and we were hemorrhaging cash, struggling to make payments. The valuation of the business and the size of the loans were based on much higher revenues and profits: We were clearly in trouble.

I closely watched the bank account every day and often moved money from a line of credit to make sure checks didn't bounce. Payday came around way too quickly, and I would lie awake at night wondering how we would make payroll. The line of credit balance got bigger and bigger as bills piled up. My employees already lacked confidence in me, so I did not feel like I had anyone to talk to in the business to improve things . . . I was alone on an island. It was a dark time for me. A time of worry, anxiety, and sleeplessness. Fortunately, there were also moments of light that gave me hope and the strength to move forward, despite a very gloomy outlook. On one occasion, we did a simple oil change for a customer, but when he came to pick up his Volvo, it would not start. He was infuriated, accusing us of breaking his car and asking what we were going to do about it. We calmly told him we would be happy to look into it for him. Our mechanics worked on a solution all day but could not find the reason for the starting failure. At the end of the day, the customer came back and demanded his car be towed to a dealership where "they knew what they were doing." Desperate to find a solution, I asked him for one more day to fix the problem and he agreed. That night, I prayed fervently that we would be able to solve this mystery so as to avoid the high cost of sending it over to the dealership.

The next morning as we opened the store, Jake from the quick lube shop down the street dropped off a car for us to work on. He overheard us talking about the Volvo and said he would be happy to help us look for a solution. He went back to his shop and returned with some electrical reading equipment. Within five minutes, he found an electrical short in a line behind the engine. He opened a cover to reveal a wire that had been pinched during a previous repair and was now completely severed. The line was in an enclosed area nowhere near the oil pan, so we knew we had not caused the failure. We installed some new wiring, and ten minutes later the car started just fine. I called the customer and told him what we found and that we would not charge him for the repair. He was satisfied with this arrangement, and we managed to save the relationship with him.

Rewarding experiences like these, where we all worked as a team and focused on making the customer happy or where a kind business neighbor chose to lend a hand, were what kept me going—despite declining bank balances—and gave me the motivation to try to save the company.

But to save the company, I knew I had to either increase revenue or cut costs. The principles of increasing revenue still eluded me, so I decided to cut costs. Reviewing payroll, I saw that I had a few employees who were very experienced and very expensive. At that time, I did not see value in my people—I only saw cost. So I let go of some of our top-paid mechanics and sales associates. Yes, our costs went down immediately, but sales crashed at an even faster rate. I was shocked when the company continued to burn through cash. I had a business doing millions of dollars of revenue, yet I had no money. The people I hired to replace those I had let go were attractive to me because they were cheap . . . and I got exactly what I paid for. These new reps wandered around the facility and ignored phone calls. When they did talk to customers, they were rude and grumpy. There was no sense of urgency, no drive to meet a goal. Veteran employees did not like me and were not excited about our direction. The energy in the

9th South store matched the economy: dark and gloomy. It became obvious to me that the atmosphere was all wrong, but I could not change company culture on my own. Thankfully, a force much more powerful than me interceded in that desperate time, connecting me with a young guy who taught me a lesson that changed everything.

It's Not About the Mangos

Even if I didn't have enough automotive experience to be running a tire store, I had learned enough from some of my previous business ventures to know that the only possible way to climb out of the hole I had dug was to find people to help me. And I didn't just want any people: I wanted the best people I could find. And I knew I would need to pay them whatever I had to in order to get them to join me. Of course, I had no money, so this was a huge leap of faith, but I was not going to tell them that. I figured if having a gloomy crew got me into trouble, then a positive, energetic team should help me dig out. So I began focusing all my energy on finding good people with optimistic attitudes. Such individuals were going to save the business— not another line of credit, and not another loan.

During my search, I heard about a young guy who was supposedly one of the top tire salespeople in the area: Jose Cordova. He was not happy with his employer at the time and was interested in a change. At age 27, he had already been with this company (which was a very good one) for ten years. He was exceptional at his job, he knew it, and he wanted to get paid to leave. We worked out a deal, which was quite a bit higher than I was paying my other salespeople. This was a scary move: *What if he isn't that good? What if I convince him to take a chance with me and we go out of business?*

Jose's infectiously positive energy soon calmed my fears. He laughed, he joked, he hustled, and most of all he cared. He cared about results, he cared about quality, and he cared about building relationships with customers.

Other members of the team did not like working with Jose—his attitude annoyed them. His vibe clashed with our dreary culture. He dominated the sales floor. Even as the new guy, his sales quickly climbed to the top, and that was threatening to some of the others. He was selling so much that we couldn't get the work done, and we needed more, highly-skilled technicians in the shop.

I learned from Jose that as a young boy he had moved from the United States to Zacatecas, Mexico, to work in his family's produce business. At age eight, he started selling mangos and other seasonal fruit. After Jose completed sixth grade, his dad said he was ready for full-time work because he could read and write, and Jose never returned to school.

Jose employed a variety of sales techniques to sell his fruit. Sometimes, he worked the family's little stand in the market, and sometimes, he carried a case of mangos to nearby traffic intersections to sell them. Other times, he went to soccer fields and sold fresh, ripe mangos sprinkled with chili powder to the players and fans. On Fridays and Saturdays, he had to sell one ton of mangos, which was a couple dozen cases weighing close to 2,000 pounds. No matter the sales method Jose used, his family had one rule: He could not stop working that day until he sold all the fruit, because if it did not sell, it would spoil. With Jose's outgoing personality, sales came naturally, and the challenge of doing it successfully became a joy to him. Work at the market started at 5 a.m. and usually went until 6 p.m. After selling produce, he returned home to help his mom throughout the evening with the family's deli, which was operated in the front of their house. This work went on every day, seven days a week.

Soon customers began seeking out Jose, in particular, in order to buy fruit from him. I asked Jose about how he was able to do so well: "How were you able to sell more mangos? Were the mangos bigger? Was your product better?"

"No," he told me.

"You must have had a lower price?" I asked.

"No, Kent. It's not about the mangos," he stated frankly with a smile.

He then explained to me that the market had many fruit vendors, all selling the same mangos at about the same price. The difference was that he worked to make friends with his customers. Naturally friendly and inquisitive, Jose would ask them about their family, their children, and their work. He made funny remarks to people as they passed and made them laugh. He commented on their hat or their shirt and tried to build a positive connection, even if it was simple and brief. In time, customers lined up to wait to buy from him, while other nearby mango vendors looked on jealously. Jose then made a statement that was a powerful spark of enlightenment for me, like a light bulb going on in my head: "It's not about what you're selling: It's all about connections. It's all about people!"

Between his naturally positive energy and a desire to build relationships, Jose became a powerhouse salesperson, not only in Mexico with his family's fruit stand but after he moved back to the United States at age 17 to work at a large chain of tire stores, where he rose to the top quickly. Again, his success came because of his positive energy and ability to spark connections. Seeing how Jose made a difference by helping me dig out of my troubles through his optimistic approach toward others spurred me to continue seeking out more top-notch people, which ultimately led to a complete turnaround of the 9th South store and to the creation of a vibrant business culture in which everyone loved to work.

Having started up multiple business ventures, beginning in my early twenties, I have learned what to do; but more importantly, I have learned what *not* to do. Of course I made some big mistakes,

Jose

one of them being my decision to let go of team players at the Big O store who could have helped me immensely in the first few months and years of running the franchise. Fortunately, I have been willing to learn from those mistakes, taking cues from such dynamos as Jose Cordova, and with a little luck I have also been blessed with some great success.

From a small scrapbooking company I started with my sister that had only a few other associates, to our large Big O Tires franchises employing hundreds of workers, I have learned that it's always the people who make the difference. I have learned that all of my potential success is not a function of my own knowledge or intellect but rather how well I understand this one crucial concept: **People matter.**

> Organizational success (and personal success, for that matter) is always based on how much you are willing to value other people, to lift them up, to connect with them, and to ensure the collective success of those on your team— as well as the customers you serve—by working together to accomplish something great.

Valuing employees, customers, and other business associates creates a healthy company culture and brings purpose and meaning into the work you do. Setting up a vibrant, thriving business climate is based largely on the quality of the people you surround yourself with and how well you treat them.

Esteeming people has taught me that things go so much better when I see the amazing value each person can offer. When I recognize the strengths each individual brings to the table, I am more willing to be patient, and I am more willing to be kind. I see that I need them, and I see that the only way my company can be one of the best organizations out there is if I embrace the merit that each person brings to the table.

Seeing the worth of others has also allowed me to make better business decisions as I have taken on new projects. When it comes to new ventures, jumping into the unknown is something required of all entrepreneurs. Frankly, it's something I'm fairly good at—and is now something I actually enjoy. It gives me energy and motivation to grow and figure out solutions, but it is not for everyone. In real life, there are best practices and there are mistakes, and I've made my fair share of both of them as I've already confessed!

Some will insist on a more measured approach. I can't argue against having as much information as possible before jumping into a business venture, but I have also seen people frozen in time, eternally analyzing whether a new idea will pay off, not daring to risk because of the fear of the unknown. And I get that. Even after some good, established success, my wife still gets queasy and expresses genuine concern when I suggest we buy another business! However, regardless of your risk tolerance (whether you prefer the risk of being an owner or the stability of being a manager), this principle will always hold true:

The people you partner with, the people you hire, the people you train, the people you encourage, and the people you elevate are what make the difference and what will ultimately make your organization successful.

This is something I know to be true deep down inside: People matter. That fact is as true for you as it is for me and has the power to transform your organization. I believe this is true for you even if your company is at the lowest point it's ever been. It's true even if you don't think you have the means to surround yourself with quality people. It's conceivable even if you've laid off the wrong people, burned bridges, or alienated those who you should have kept the closest. It's true even if you have stopped believing in yourself.

The power that valuing people can have on your company culture and ultimately on your success cannot be overstated. As FranklinCovey CEO Robert Whitman has observed, "Nearly everything about your organization—including your strategy, products, and systems—can be replaced, except one thing: the effectiveness of your people. Culture is the ultimate competitive advantage."

Throughout the pages of this book, I want to share with you the enormous impact that having the right people around me has had on my business (and on the organizations of others) and what it can potentially do for yours as well. You will see how I have learned to adapt, how I have learned to value people so much more than I did initially, and the tremendous influence our team now has on me, on both a personal and professional level. You will see how I learned that my potential success is not a function of my own knowledge or intellect, but rather is based on how well I create a team, effectively work with that team to build others up, and glean important knowledge by being open to the light within others. Making a connection makes all the difference.

If you are outside my industry, you might not think of tire shops as a place to model positive, dynamic corporate culture, but we have proven that this type of culture can be achieved in any organization. I hope what I have learned about the following topics we will cover in this book will help you in your efforts to create a better company culture wherein everyone can flourish:

- How great people bring great light to an organization;
- Why building people up then builds up your business;

- Why avoiding cheap labor matters so much;
- Why it's important to find people who enjoy work and who believe they influence their own outcomes; and
- Why little things are big things when it comes to connecting with some of the most important people in your business: your customers.

I love what Malcolm Forbes has said about the importance of valuing people, no matter what circumstance you find yourself in: "Too many people overvalue what they are not, and undervalue what they are." All people have a light within them. In some individuals, this light seems to be a small spark; in others, it is a blazing spotlight! In the next chapter, I will focus on the importance of finding people with this great light.

1

Great People Bring Light

"Give light, and people will find the way."
—Ella Baker

Hiring Jose Cordova was, indeed, one of the best things I did to help turn things around at the 9th South store. He brought tremendous light into a dark and dismal place and helped spur me on to surround myself with other proactive people who could make a difference.

The team was now beginning to gel a bit more and had more desire. Positive energy was starting to return to the shop. I told my team that we would someday get back to the $6 million in sales the previous owner had achieved in 2006. And they believed me. As sales continued to climb, I continued to learn the importance of valuing people and building a team filled with those who seemed to be lit up inside.

While the concept of there being "light" within people may seem esoteric and mystical to some, is a very real notion to me. The light each of us possesses can give tremendous strength and hope.

Each of us is so much more than what we see on the surface. There is something within all of us that is of infinite worth, and when we look for that value in others and in ourselves, that light becomes more apparent and we begin to understand that there is more to each of us than a mere set of skills to be utilized or cast aside.

When we ignore the light, we work in darkness, and that awful darkness spreads to others. I have seen examples of this darkness in organizational managers, and the negative effect it has on a business can be devastating. Right after finishing college, I was working as an accountant for a waste management company in California, and the site manager there was really hard on people. The office manager, who was a very reliable woman, lived in constant fear of being reprimanded by this supervisor. When he needed her to input a pile of paperwork, he would march to her desk and say, "I need these put in the system within the hour," then intentionally drop the pile onto the floor rather than setting it on her desk. He would then turn on his heel and leave her to pick up the papers and complete the task. He had no light. There is no place for such people in an organization that wants to succeed.

On the other hand, when we embrace light, it shines brighter in ourselves and we are able to recognize it more fully in others. Seeking out individuals who readily give off this light or positive energy is vital if you are going to build a business culture where people matter. As I mentioned in the introduction, the people you partner with, hire, train, encourage, and elevate are what make the difference and will ultimately affect whether your organization takes off or not. I have found success when I am striving to seek greater light in myself and when I work to surround myself with people who have light as well.

I See the Light

Building a team of people who had positive energy allowed us to start climbing out of the hole I had dug for myself when I first took on the business in 2006. By 2013, sales had risen to $4.5 million, and the next year we hit $4.9 million. With a little more money and a lot more confidence in the game plan, I became fixated on finding more great people. I was able to coax back Robbie Carter, the top salesperson I mentioned in the introduction who had left when I first bought the 9th South store. We were so fortunate to have him return to our team: Robbie's optimistic attitude and positive energy are second to none. He has never met a challenge he doesn't want to annihilate, whether it be diagnosing an elusive vehicle issue or attacking a sand dune by launching over it in a side-by-side UTV. He always does things full-bore, with enthusiasm.

Robbie's energy contributed heavily to our sales exploding over-night. Everyone in the store could feel his influence—just as they had felt Jose Cordova's—from crew members to customers. Employees who did not want to jump into the new healthy, upbeat culture we were creating weeded themselves out. Then Robbie's hard-working, focused brother, Reese Carter, joined us as well and added yet another solid building block to the new, positive culture we were creating. The Carters are the perfect example of the type of powerhouse people you want to attract to your business.

Robbie, who is now the 9th South store manager, has a relentless optimism that inspires everyone on the team. He is hard-working and genuinely kind. He cares about the success of the business and about the people in the organization.

I have worked with Robbie for many years now, and he starts every single day with a smile. Every Monday morning, as we get ready to begin a new week, he gives me a high-five and asks, "Do you know what today is?" I already know the answer, considering we've done this routine hundreds of times now, but I ask, "What?" anyway.

He answers, "It's make-it-happen-Monday!" On Tuesday, when I first get to the shop, I ask him something like, "How are things looking today?" The inevitable answer is, "Great! It's make-it-happen-Tuesday!" (And so on, every day of the week.) His positivity is so over-the-top it's borderline annoying. And I love it. Robbie has light. The reason that energy is so powerful is because it radiates from him very naturally. He's not just saying those words; he really means them. His attitude remains pretty constant, no matter how bad the day before might have been or what challenges lie ahead. It is just part of him.

His brother, Reese, has a different personality, but he shines just as brightly as Robbie, and his light also lifts our organization. While Robbie is known for his unwavering optimism, Reese is a tireless worker. He has tracked how many steps he walks at work for years and has found that they add up to an average of eight to ten miles a day. Although he is not as vocal as his brother, Reese leads by example.

A few years ago, one of our stores was struggling to increase sales. No matter what we tried, we could not get the leadership team to buy into our sales program. They seemed to be satisfied with being just okay. We tried contests, financial incentives, and prizes. And when those didn't work we even tried warnings and ultimatums. But nothing in those few years and multiple managers seemed to move the needle.

I don't typically like to blame a lack of success on problems that seem to be out of our control. To me, there's no point in blaming the location, economy, or weather; these issues are not what most affect our business. It's always us: the people. But I was starting to doubt this theory. Perhaps this store really was in a bad location after all, and the only solution was to move it. Or maybe we just didn't have the right people working there. Needing to find answers, I decided to do a test.

I knew that if anyone in our organization could make an immediate positive impact on a store, it was Reese. I sent him to this shop, asking him to help me understand if there was an intrinsic problem with the location, the crew of workers, or maybe the customers. He only had one week to determine if the store had potential or not. Without hesitation or complaint, he drove an extra hour each way to work at this location. He did not know a single employee, he had no history with any of the customers, and he did not know the area.

The first day he was there, I introduced Reese to the crew, and in his very succinct but positive way he said, "This week is going to be great. We have a great facility, we have customers, and I know we can do great things here. We just have to choose to be great." That was it. Then he walked quickly away and started setting up for the day. I loved his use of the word "we" as he greeted the crew. As a visitor for only one week, he could have easily kept himself detached from that group, but he saw the value in making himself one with them.

After he was settled, Reese approached each employee and took time to get to know them a little bit. Within 30 minutes, the crew pretty much understood that Reese was going to take the store to another level—and they seemed excited about this. You could feel that excitement; it was palpable. The team took to Reese's enthusiasm because they wanted to be great, and deep down they knew they could be. People with light are able to bring the light in others to the surface and make them strong and confident in their abilities.

Before Reese got to that store, the average revenue per day was $5,652. But on the first Monday Reese began working with the team, the store brought in $12,810 and then averaged over $12,000 in sales per day the rest of the week.

After this test period, Reese met with me to advise me on what he had observed at that location. It was a glowing report. He said the customers were fun and easy to work with, the building was perfect, and the employees were knowledgeable and hard-working. "There is no reason that store couldn't double sales immediately with the right leadership," he told me. Management with positive energy was what that location needed. What happened after he left, when the store immediately went back to its $5,800 daily average, only further proved to me that it's the people that matter, not the location, the product, the economy, the weather, or the customers. A person with light, like Reese, can have an immediate and meaningful impact on an organization, and not everyone can replicate it easily.

Both Robbie and Reese are crazy men (in a good way!). Whenever the Carters go on a trek across some of the thousands of miles of Utah trails, I wonder if they will come back alive! Coming from a family of five brothers, they've never met an adventure they didn't like. And, similar to how they approach challenges at work, they have a knack for and seem to seek out demanding and sometimes even dicey situations that they can try to tackle. From the steep, forested mountain terrain of northern Utah to the sagebrush and sand dunes of the West Desert to the Mars-like red rock of southern Utah, they chase it all.

Robbie says if you don't get stuck somewhere, you don't get to figure out how to get out. Can-do attitudes like these are part of what makes the Carters such a great asset to our company. Their willingness to pitch in and help where help is needed, whether at work or out on one of their many adventures, shows that they have light within them.

Reese demonstrated this light while out driving a UTV with his wife and two daughters on a long trail near the Grand Canyon a few years back. They came upon a family in distress: another guy in a UTV had taken a turn too sharply and driven off the road and down into a ravine. He and his machine were both badly damaged. His family was trying to help him, but his injuries were serious enough that he needed medical attention or he might not survive. Reese and his wife and daughters took off in their UTV to seek higher ground and hopefully a cell phone connection. After going dozens of miles as fast as they could, Reese called emergency services to give them the GPS coordinates of the accident, and a Life Flight helicopter was sent in.

Having gone way out of their way to help the distressed group, Reese and his family started to make their way back to Mesquite, Nevada, but ran out of gas 30 miles from town. The desert got cold very quickly when the sun went down, and he and his family huddled together with a couple of blankets for five hours in very chilly 40-degree weather. Reese was eventually able to connect with Robbie, who drove out to give his brother fuel at 3 a.m.

The Carters are often the first people others think of when help is needed. A few years ago, one of our 9th South team members was driving from Utah to Denver and had a bad accident. He hit a patch of ice in a remote area of central Wyoming and rolled his SUV, with his family inside. Miraculously, no one was seriously injured, but there was no one nearby to help them. Not knowing what else to do, the associate called Robbie on a Saturday morning and told him what had happened. Robbie immediately got his truck and trailer and set off for Wyoming. Six hours later, the family was in Robbie's truck, and the damaged vehicle was on the trailer. Everyone arrived home safely that night.

I hear about stories like these involving the Carters all the time, and each one is an inspiring example of how they make things happen. If you are in a bind, there is no one else you would rather have on your team (or on your trail!) than Reese and Robbie Carter. They bring light and optimism to every situation.

Robbie   Reese

During my quest to find people of light, in addition to the Carters and Jose Cordova, I was also able to bring a great mechanic with an amazing attitude on board: Jose Rizo. "Rizo," as he is known in our shop, brings a positive vibe to our organization by rallying our technician team. He demonstrated this proactive attitude one evening a while back when a customer was passing through Salt Lake City on his way home to Nevada from a long business trip. The customer stopped in our store because his vehicle was making major rattling noises and the brakes were not working right. We diagnosed a myriad of safety issues that would require about ten hours of labor less than an hour before we were closing for the day.

When Rizo heard the plight of the man, who desperately wanted to get back to Nevada that night for an event with his children the next morning, he gathered his team of mechanics and said, "I will be staying tonight as long as it takes so this man can get home to his family. Anyone who wants to help me can." Six technicians jumped in and started to work. There was a technician on each corner of the car and one under the hood assisted by a helper. Together, they

Back: Javier, Jeremy, "Rizo", Emigdio, Alex; Front: Rogelio

were able to fast-track the service and sent the man on his way about 90 minutes after our regular closing time. While talking on his cell phone, the customer got a bit emotional as he told his wife what we had done. People with light have a desire to make someone's day, even when they don't have to.

Many other members of our team have amazing character, like one of our best technicians, Gerardo Murillo. The following incident illustrates his ability to bring positive energy into our organization.

One of our customers had new tires installed at a competitor's store in an emergency on his limousine, which he used for driving people around on special occasions. One evening, shortly after the new tires had been put on his vehicle, the limo was hired by the parents of a 15-year-old girl for her quinceañera party. The young lady, her parents, and her friends were enjoying a ride to the party in the limo when the vehicle abruptly stopped. Because of a valve-stem error during the tire installation, two of the four brand-new tires had gone completely flat, leaving the party-goers stranded and distraught, worrying about all the people awaiting their arrival at the party.

The business where the limo owner had purchased the tires could not help, so he called us. He asked if there was anything we could do, even though he had bought the tires elsewhere and it was pretty late in the day, near closing time.

One of our sales associates called Gerardo, who lived near where the limo had broken down, and asked if he could help. Since Gerardo is always willing to help, he loaded up some equipment and headed out to assist the group. It didn't matter to Gerardo that he had to work in 100-degree summer heat on his day off: he didn't hesitate to jump in, and soon had the party-goers back on the road.

Gerardo

Attracting People Who Have Light into Your Business

An August 2019 article in *Automotive News* highlights why it is so important these days to attract people who can bring a positive vibe into your shop: "Because [customers] can find the same deals . . . in just a few clicks on the internet, your employees are critical to winning over new customers—and keeping them."

Online shopping and buying options are so prevalent today across all industries, even in the tire and automotive services market, that counting on attracting customers based on product features or even price is not going to be enough. Remember, it's not about the mangos. Making connections with your customers in a way that helps them feel comfortable buying from you rather than from the slew of other options they have right at their fingertips is now essential. And making those connections requires that you attract and train people who have light and that you value these people in order to keep them on your team.

I have often been asked how I have managed to find energetic, enthusiastic people like Jose Cordova and the Carter brothers. There are five personality traits that indicate to me that a potential hire is likely a person of light. I look for these traits when recruiting or hiring someone for our organization. These things do not guarantee a great result, but they work for me much of the time.

They Smile

A simple, genuine smile goes a long way. While I know great people who rarely look happy, and smiley people who I wouldn't want in my organization, I have found that individuals with an authentic smile tend to be energetic people who are lit from within.

They Are Interested in Others

People with light ask questions about me (they don't just talk about themselves), and they listen to my answers. Being curious and asking questions can indicate a keen interest in other people. When they sit back and listen carefully to my answers, I know the person is likely someone I want in my organization. As Oliver Wendall Holmes advised in his 1883 classic, *The Poet at the Breakfast Table*, "It is the province of knowledge to speak, and it is the privilege of wisdom to listen." In my opinion, listening is a skill that indicates light because it shows empathy and sensibility.

They Are Confident but Also Have Humility

A great balance of confidence and humility can indicate light. People with this balance recognize their own merit. They know they have something to offer and are willing to give it openly. Their humility allows them to share their strengths without dominating or belittling others. They understand they have flaws, just like everyone else, but they often use their confidence to build up others without operating out of fear that they will appear weak.

They Have Strength to Move Past Their Failures

I have found that brightly lit people, while aware of their failures, are also able to move past them and can recognize how they have improved as people because of them.

We all have failures, yet I am always amazed by the people I interview who have no recognition of their own faults (at least none they admit). This can indicate a lack of light because they seem to have no basic self-awareness. This disconnect from their flaws makes them much less likely to be teachable, which in my opinion is one of the worst problems a person can have. Famed American author Og Mandino said, "Take the attitude of a student, never be too big to ask questions, never know too much to learn something new."

Some people take the awareness of their faults too far and focus too much on past mistakes. They beat themselves up for their failures and hold on to the darkness this brings into their lives unnecessarily. The sweet spot is right in the middle: a person who is aware of past mistakes, has learned from them, and has moved forward. This indicates emotional maturity and someone who understands that there is a learning process to life. These individuals are much more likely to be teachable and trainable and will be more patient and forgiving of others' mistakes.

They Don't Blame Others

Excuses are very unattractive to me, and they seem to block the light. The 14th Dalai Lama has said, "The key to happiness is peace of mind. This is not something that can be bought. Inner peace has to be cultivated by each of us from within." Being able to recognize that each of us controls how we choose to feel, how we choose to react, and how we choose to spend each moment of our day is a powerful character trait which, to me, indicates great light.

While none of these attributes I have shared seem to mean too much in isolation, if a person has all or most of these characteristics, I know I am on the right track and can have confidence that bringing them into our organization is going to be a win for everyone.

In addition to what I've learned about being able to recognize and attract people with light, here are a few more tips for finding people who can bring energy to your business, as noted in the *Automotive News* article I cited earlier:

Create a Strong Company Culture

According to Evelyn Rojos of Fox Motors in Chicago, who was quoted in the *Automotive News* article, "Recruiting [the right people] starts at the top. You have to have the right culture . . . to entice the right people to join your team. [You must build a culture] with a lot of intention, about how you speak to each other, how employees work with customers, how they talk about other departments."

It's important that you believe in your own company culture and live by it. Former employees talk about their experiences at your organization, so if you are not being genuine in creating a culture that truly does value people, that expects everyone in the business to treat others with respect, and that is working for the collective success of all involved, that reputation will follow you. It's best to be honest in the way you conduct business and the way you expect your team to conduct themselves around each other and with the customer. It is important that everyone buys into the concept of radiating light as much as possible.

Former Starbucks chairman and CEO Howard Schultz affirmed this in his book, *Pour Your Heart into It,* when he wrote, "Whatever your culture, your values, your guiding principles, you have to take steps to inculcate them into the organization early in its life so that they can guide every decision, every hire, every strategic objective you set."

Work on Your Own Leadership Skills

The 2019 *Automotive News* article explains why your own leadership skills are so important if you want to have the right people in your shop: "Fleming Ford, vice president of people analytics at ESI Trends, a Florida consulting firm . . . underscores the importance of top leaders in attracting and keeping good workers. 'General managers have to get better at the people part—explaining the vision, inspiring the team,' she says. 'They've got to get over the idea that they're selling cars [or tires or mangos or whatever else]; their job is to manage the people who sell [these things].' Ford suggests a daily huddle with managers reinforcing different core values."

My take on this is that reinforcing core values is fine, so long as you really believe in them yourself and really live them in your company; otherwise, these daily huddles become nothing more than empty, rah-rah pep rallies that do nothing to help your people make a difference in your organization. As Mark Wetterau, the chairman and CEO of food manufacturer and distribution giant Golden State Foods, has so aptly observed, "If you make a commitment to a [set of values], it's a never-ending endeavor. You've got to constantly not only keep them front and center and talk about them, but you've got to live them and demonstrate them throughout the entire organization. It needs to flow not only from the CEO, but to all the leadership all the way down to mid-management to the supervisors to the folks on the floor."

When you are interviewing potential hires who have come highly recommended, communicating your core values and the way the company expects top recruits to function can be a great way to assess how a potential employee responds to such values. If they don't seem all that interested in your values, then you know they may not be a person who has what it takes to be part of your company. Ask them pointed questions about what they would do in certain situations, how they would respond to specific problems in your organization, and how they would treat a fellow associate in a particular circumstance. How the potential employee responds to these questions can be very telling and help you discern what type of character the person has.

In conclusion, I want to share with you some wise words by an amazing inspirational speaker, Jason Hall, who also happens to be my brother-in-law. At age 15, Jason broke his neck jumping into a lake and became paralyzed from the chest down: "Learn to SEE GOOD. Work to DO GOOD. Live to BE GOOD."

Before his death in 2019, Jason traveled the world, influencing people with many such powerful words and sharing the reasons he chose to face daily challenges caused by his disability with positive energy rather than self-pity. As my brother-in-law, he has had a huge impact on my life. If there is anyone on this planet who has embodied the idea of light, it is Jason.

To me, Jason's attitude is the perfect example of someone filled with vibrant optimism. People like Jason, and many of the wonderful associates I am privileged to work with on my team at Big O Tires, have truly made a difference in the world. Their drive and enthusiasm bring light to everyone they are involved with.

If you find yourself mired down in a gloomy company culture where it's hard to see the light, I hope what I have shared in this chapter about the importance of finding the right people to help you succeed has hit home in some way. I hope you will do what it takes to attract and retain people of light so you can create a healthy business environment, one that brings purpose and meaning into the work you do.

In the next chapter, I will outline why it is so important—once you have found the right people—to build them up so they can build up your organization.

2

Build People Up, and They Will Build Up the Organization

"You can't build a great building on a weak foundation. You must have a solid foundation if you're going to have a superstructure."

—Gordon B. Hinckley

Two of the most brutal weeks of my fairly coddled teenage life were spent on a hillside in Pleasant View, Utah, harvesting cherries. If you are a farmer or rancher, please disregard this story because I know there is no chance you could possibly feel bad for me. You do the type of work I'm about to describe in your sleep, never complaining about it. But for anyone who doesn't have firsthand knowledge of how hard farm work can be, believe me, it was torture.

When I was 14, I worked on the "shaker crew" for the Listons, my brother-in-law's family, who owned a fruit orchard operation. The job began on a July evening around 10 p.m. when some other workers and

I met to take a pickup ride along Canal Road to shake some cherry trees. We worked all night, and then another crew started in the early morning and did their shift. The job was difficult and was best done at night to avoid the hot Utah summer afternoons.

To do the work, two of us crouched on the edge of the harvester as it chugged along the rows of trees, pulled by a tractor. When the tractor had aligned the harvester so that it was even with the tree trunk, we jumped off and pulled a large, heavy tarp around the base of the tree. This by itself wouldn't have been too bad, but there were some obstacles.

First, as the harvester chugged along, the branches of the trees whipped and scratched our faces and arms. When we jumped off with the tarp in tow, we had to close our eyes and just go for it, as the branches further beat across our faces. Second, the orchard was on a hill and the tarp quickly felt very heavy as we pulled it up the incline.

Once the tarp was in place, we had a few seconds to rest while another tractor moved in, hooked onto the tree, and shook it. Hundreds of cherries fell onto the tarp. As the harvester began rolling up the tarp, we then had to pull the now heavier tarp taut so it could be rolled up properly by the harvester. As we walked back to the tractor, we were again whipped in the face with tree branches. When the tarp was completely rolled up, we hopped back on the harvester and moved to the next tree. Looking down that long row and knowing we had to repeat the back-breaking work of pulling that heavy tarp up the hill, I sometimes got so tired I wanted to quit: I did not think I could pull the tarp one more time.

When I returned home after the first day of work and sat on the porch steps of my house, I could not believe I had made it through that night. I determined that I was going to quit. My oldest sister, Kara, who is married to one of the Liston boys, came out and asked me how it went. I told her I was going to quit. She told me that I couldn't: They needed me. I had to stick it out and not make our family look bad. So I begrudgingly agreed.

That night I showed up at the pickup truck with my lunch sack full of three peanut butter and grape jelly sandwiches to continue the torture. During this shift, we began sorting all the cherries that had been shaken from the trees. On the back side of the harvester, we worked in a sorting crew, a few of us watching as the cherries fell into bins. We then picked out the branches and leaves and carried the full bins to dump into the "tanker," a large container full of water. This wasn't as exhausting as pulling the tarp, but it wasn't very enjoyable either, as every insect in the orchard was attracted to the lights of the equipment and continually buzzed in our ears and eyes.

As the last day of harvest approached, I became so excited. I knew I could survive one more bug-filled night, and then the misery would be over. Near the end of our shift, as the sun rose, a tire got punctured on the tractor and we were stuck until the tire could be changed. We waited for about an hour, and finally Mr. Liston decided to send us home while he waited for the morning crew. As I gratefully headed to the truck, Mrs. Liston pulled me aside and whispered, "Kent, I know you're tired, but we are not going to be able to finish the harvest today unless we have some more help, so I need you to stay for the next shift." I couldn't believe what she was asking of me! I told her I was exhausted and I didn't think I could do it. She looked me in the eyes and responded, "Kent, we need you."

I stayed. But I thought I was going to die. My belly was screaming with hunger. I devoured my three peanut butter and jelly sandwiches hours earlier, and I was completely famished as the sun rose higher and the temperature with it.

They finally got the tire fixed, and the other crew showed up so we could finish the job. By the time it was done, I had worked 15 straight hours and was mad about it, but I also remember feeling very satisfied that I had survived it. More than that, however, I really liked being needed. It made me feel strong and appreciated. That night, Mrs. Liston taught me a valuable lesson about the importance of making others feel needed: She built me up, which then gave me confidence that I had more to offer.

Have you ever felt truly needed? It's a wonderful feeling when you get to experience it. Feeling needed is powerful, and is something that we all universally enjoy and desire. When business leaders and organization heads understand this—the importance of building people up in a way that makes them feel needed, wanted, and even loved—their organization will grow stronger.

Feeling needed gives people confidence, which in turn gives them motivation to improve, to add value to the work they do, and to be driven by personal initiative rather than waiting to be driven to perform. When you build people up, they will in turn build up your organization.

The entire premise of this book, as I stated in the introduction, is the fact that people matter. Your organization's success is always a function of how well you comprehend and internalize this fact and how well you are able to communicate it to those you lead, influence, and serve. In my experience, one of the best ways to ensure that the people around you know they matter is to help them see that their skills, abilities, talents, and even time are valuable to you. When they feel needed, something almost magical happens to your company culture. Where there may have been resistance and push-back against directives and work assignments, an easy, lightened-up vibe begins to take over. The need to drive, push, and threaten disappears. You may notice members of your team coming in early or even staying a bit late. Problem-solving becomes less burdensome as the effort evolves into a more natural process. There is greater cooperation and cohesiveness as team members strive to meet your positive expectations of them, wanting to please you rather than doing the bare minimum to get by. Making people feel needed promotes collaboration, the desire for mutual success, and greater purpose.

A 2017 article entitled, "The Pygmalion Effect," published in the online magazine *Potentialife*, supports the idea that company leaders can have the power to affect the way people perform based on how well they value them and whether they have high expectations of them: "A series of studies has demonstrated that leaders and authority figures play a major role in the successes or failures of the people under their supervision." The article then highlights the famous Rosenthal/Jacobson study, conducted in 1966 in a San Francisco elementary school, wherein teachers were told that about 20 percent of their students—listed by name—were expected to be "intellectual bloomers" and would have a burst of intellectual development based on results of the "Harvard Test of Infected Acquisition" the children had supposedly been given. This is what the teachers were told, but in reality there was no such exam, and the kids had only been given a standard IQ test. The names of the so-called "intellectual bloomers" had been chosen randomly.

At the end of the school year when the experiment ended, it was discovered that the students in the random sample who had been identified as better intellectual performers did, indeed, significantly outperform the other students in all subjects. It was concluded that because the teachers had been told these students were going to outperform their classmates, they then expected them to do so, treating these children differently and having higher expectations of them than their peers, which affected outcomes. When the IQ test was administered again, the children in the random sample had actually increased their IQ score significantly due to meeting the high expectations their teachers had placed upon them.

The article goes on to illustrate how this phenomenon shows up in the workplace as well: "Harvard professor J. Sterling Livingston replicated [the Rosenthal/Jacobson] findings in the workplace. Managers were told that their employees had been given a test to identify potential and were then given the names of those who had done best. But as in the Rosenthal experiment, the names had been chosen randomly. In his write-up of the study . . . Livingston noted that . . . manager's expectation had a huge impact on the performance and career progress of their employees." The article then cites leadership researchers Bruce Avolio and Fred Luthan's findings on what happens when management values their employees: "'The single most reliable indicator of how successful an employee will be, is the extent to which somebody believes in [them].'"

Loving People: A Powerful Way to Build Your Organization

Am I allowed to say the "l-word" in a business book? It may seem cheesy or corny in such a setting, but I am not really sure what other word describes this way to build people up so they can build up your organization.

In our company, we shoot for impeccable efficiency, proper sales technique, great marketing, and effective inventory management, but the presence of love in the workplace changes everything. It means that I do not want to let my team down, and they do not want to let me down. It means I communicate how much I need them, and they understand their value in the organization. Love in the workplace means:

- We speak to each other with respect, even when mistakes are made;
- We respect our customers and recognize they could choose to take their business elsewhere and that they may be going through challenges we cannot see;
- We treat our vendors as partners we need in order to be successful;
- We don't judge people based on their appearance—not everyone looks like me, was born under the same circumstances, grew up like I did, goes to the same church, or has the same kind of parents—we all bring something different to the table and that is beneficial;
- We believe that each person in our organization is going to connect with different customers in a different way and that we need that diversity and welcome it.

Let me give a personal example of how loving people in the work setting can make a huge difference. After completing an undergraduate degree from Brigham Young University and an MBA from Utah State University, I got my first professional job at BFI Waste in Salt Lake City. The job was to act as a staff accountant. I say "act as" because although my education dabbled in accounting, I was definitely no accountant!

My first day on the job, the controller, Annette, gave me a list of journal entries to complete and sent me back to my cubicle. I stared at those things and realized I was in big trouble. I had no idea how to be a staff accountant; I could not do one single journal entry. After fumbling through my first day, I spent much of that night and every night that week studying accounting. Because my brother Kory had hooked me up with this job, I worried I was going to make him look bad for getting me hired and was going to get fired from my first job out of college! It was a stressful time, considering my first child had been born just a week prior.

Fortunately, Annette was very patient with me and basically taught me accounting. The year I spent in that job changed how I would later view and understand business, and I am very grateful for Annette's patience. I don't know if she would describe her actions and the way she treated me as love, but love was at the heart of her willingness to help me.

No matter what the state of your organization right now, you can take it to another level by learning the importance of making people feel this kind of love and feel needed and valued. Potential success is not a function of your own knowledge or intellect; rather, it is based on how well you work with your team to build them up, how high you expect them to reach, and how well they then go out and build up others. Remember, when you build people up, they will in turn build up your business.

Tearing Down Does Not Build a Strong Organization

To illustrate the importance of building people up, I want to share with you what happens when you do the opposite. Unfortunately, I have made mistakes in the past with this principle. In the early days of our tire franchise, we had hired a teenage girl to drive our shop truck around to pick up parts, bill our customers, and do other odds and ends. One day, I walked into the shop to find a veteran salesperson yelling at this young woman for taking too long during an errand. He was red-faced and spewing profanities with his finger pointed at her, jabbing the air in front of her, making sure she knew without a doubt that she had made a mistake. He then turned to me and told me I had better fire her immediately for wasting company time. I am ashamed to admit it, but I didn't yet know better and did ask her to leave while she cried many tears, even though she had a reasonable explanation for what had happened. In that moment, my salesman and I were destructive. We tore down instead of building up.

Have you ever been belittled or berated by a boss or a co-worker? If so, how did that go? Let me guess . . . you hated it. From what I have witnessed in the auto maintenance industry, this type of management style seems to be the gold standard. Many people are looking to destroy rather than build up. I have seen this play out many times: the hard-nosed, top-down, "do what I tell you or you're fired" approach. Now, when I see one of my own store managers treat people badly, I am embarrassed. I then go back to the drawing board with these types of supervisors and retrain them. Part of that instruction includes showing them how to treat those who break company policy in a dignified and professional manner.

Here are some of the tamer things I have heard in other car repair shops (and in mine in the past before I quit tolerating destructive behavior). Be sure to use your imagination and add multiple curse words per sentence:

- "Don't think! You're not paid to think! Just do your job or find another one!"
- "Come to my office to talk to the person who signs your paycheck!"
- "No, you don't get a spiff (immediate bonus). You're paid to do a job, so quit if you don't like it!"
- "I don't care if it's your first day: This is common sense. You're fired!"
- "If you don't get better, you're out of here!"
- "Just work better!"

Some of the people I have worked with seem to constantly threaten their subordinates with termination. When new workers come to our stores, they often wonder why we don't fire people for small or first-time infractions. I'm not sure where this quick-to-fire thing started, but it must have originated where there is a never-ending supply of new, much better workers. In the markets where our stores are located, this would be a luxury! What I have seen is that when one person with flaws leaves, the replacement person has flaws as well, so it makes more sense to work with the first person.

Don't fire employees for small infractions. All people will make minor mistakes, so if you fire them over little offenses, you will be constantly firing people! This creates high turnover, an inexperienced workforce, and lots of unhappy customers because more mistakes will be made. Here's an example of how this can backfire on you:

The economy in our area is booming, with a lot of new construction, and it is difficult to find employees. At one point, we had hired a new tire technician, Eddie, who seemed to have a lot of promise. The manager told him to come to work the next day at 7:30 a.m. A couple of days later, I asked the manager how Eddie was doing. He told me, "Oh, he showed up at 7:32, and I'm not going to put up with that, so I fired him." I was not happy to hear this. Obviously, I had failed in my training of that manager. Watching the clock and warning someone over a minute or two feels dictator-like to me. Of course, this does not mean there are no expectations or consequences for actual infractions, which I will explain later in the chapter, but getting worked up about little things is no way to build people up so they can help you build up your business.

Here are a few things to keep in mind that I believe are worth living by if you want to create a culture within your organization that promotes low turnover and the mutual success of everyone involved in your venture.

Never Belittle People

Charles Dickens has said that we should, "Think of people below [us] as if they were really fellow passengers to the grave, and not another race of creatures bound on other journeys." I like the principle, but I take it a step further by trying to put everyone on an equal playing field rather than looking at anyone as "below" another. From a humanistic perspective, other people are not below me, and I am not above them. Yes, I have employees who report to me, but we are all "fellow passengers to the grave."

Here are some of the phrases I have found to be effective at making people feel needed; building people up rather than tearing them down; and creating a positive, collaborative environment where team members take responsibility for their actions without me hovering over them:

- "Thank you for what you did today."
- "I am glad I am on your team."
- "You have strengths that we need."
- "Thanks for taking the initiative on this, it helped out a lot."
- I really appreciate the thoughtful problem-solving."

Yelling Is Not an Effective Method for Achieving Lasting Behavioral Change

Raising your voice does nothing but create contempt. People will tune out yelling and go back to bad behavior as soon as the screamer's back is turned or try to figure out ways to get around the person so they can avoid being treated so disrespectfully.

I have a colleague who, right out of college, took a job with a company whose founder was a tyrant notorious for his angry outbursts. She said sometimes he would berate her so intensely she could see the veins in his temples pounding violently and she had to dodge the spit spewing from his mouth. She wondered if he would have a stroke or a heart attack right there while yelling at her. The culture at that company was toxic, and employees lived in fear and dread.

Unless there is an urgent safety hazard to take heed of, like a fire, there is no need ever to raise your voice to those who work for you. Most people who are parents have had to learn this the hard way at home, so it should come as no surprise that the same principle applies at work. I have found that in the long run, yelling doesn't work and that people begin to tune out someone who constantly raises their voice. I choose not to berate others with obscenities, which can be common in the vehicle repair business. I would hate for someone to put me down or be in my face all the time, yelling at me. I can't imagine other people wanting that from me or wanting to help me build a great company if that was the typical course of action I took with them.

Stop Expecting the Worst

Just like parents are urged to believe in their children in order to help them grow into happy, functioning adults who can contribute to society, business owners, executives, and organization heads should believe in the people who work for them and with them as well. Anne Shiess, a parenting author, said in her book, *Got Kids?*, "Believing in your children, really believing in them, will compensate for the many mistakes you will make with them." In the same way, choosing to believe in the people who work with you will make up for a multitude of deficiencies, both yours and theirs.

When I have a flawed person with a positive attitude and a desire to learn and get better, I will give that person many chances. I believe most people want to become better, want to feel good about their contributions, and want to feel needed. It is the leader's job to provide an environment where that can happen. In our shops, rather than falling back on the easy thing to do—get frustrated, raise your voice, and issue threats—we have tried to take a different approach by helping our associates feel needed, which sort of naturally helps them progress and reach their goals without excessive pressure on our part.

Don't Expect Perfection

I am very aware of my own mistakes, so I operate under the assumption that others will make mistakes also. But I have found that most errors are made because leadership does not put a system in place that allows team members to succeed. If people on my team are continually making the same mistakes, I have to look in the mirror and see where I have failed. What system did I not implement correctly? What training did I skip? Eric Ries, author of *The Lean Startup*, said, "Remember, most mistakes are caused by flawed systems, not bad people."

The people we work with and associate with are running their own race and will reap the rewards of their own progress. I'm not talking about a "medals-for-all" philosophy, regardless of effort. I'm saying that everyone is moving through life at their own pace, and we must never expect them to run faster than they can or to do things exactly the way we do them in order to be acceptable. Expecting perfection in ourselves or others is a recipe for disaster. When people fail, and they will, we do not need to be so harsh (as noted in the previous section). I believe in allowing others to be and feel successful at their own level—to be able to stand tall where they are at that moment if they are giving it their best. Expecting everyone in the organization to achieve the same level of success at the same time is unreasonable.

When you let people have a win within their own skillset and abilities, whatever they are, they will build on that success and become better, thus rising to the next level where they can work to achieve and be even more. This cycle for success gets repeated over and over until people have become masters and experts in their field and can be given greater responsibilities and meet higher expectations. Let your team members grow and improve at the rate at which they are most likely to succeed. This helps build them up and helps them feel needed, which then gives them the incentive to want to do more for you and for your organization.

Take a moment now to think about the way you treat the people you work with. Do you look down on them, belittle them, or expect them to be perfect? If so, I urge you to determine a better way of approaching your relationship with them. Choose instead to believe in them, to let them succeed at their own pace, to respect the skills and talents they bring to the table, to have faith that they can overcome their flaws, and to trust that they have what it takes to help make your company stronger. Remember, people will rise to the level of expectation that you give them, as was demonstrated in the Rosenthal/Jacobson experiment I highlighted earlier in this chapter.

Building People Up Builds a Positive Culture

As I brought more people with light into the 9th South store, as I mentioned in chapter 1—people like Jose Cordova, Rizo, and Gerardo—more associates began to join us who wanted to build others up as well, and the culture really started to change in a lot of amazing ways. The entire team began to catch on to the new, positive energy in the shop, and focused more on building each other up. A number of years ago, this was demonstrated in spades when one of our technicians was diagnosed with stomach cancer. After losing 50 pounds very quickly and not being able to eat, he was in very bad shape. He missed months of work, and many of the employees banded together to give the family food and money for expenses. As a unified group, the company became united to provide a wonderful Christmas for Mom, Dad, and their children. The team's message to this associate was, "Get better because we need you."

This was an experience that connected our team closer to each other. Fortunately, the employee beat the ugly cancer and still works for us today as an experienced mechanic. I am not saying that building others up and making them feel needed will always cure everything, cancer included, but it did bring light and hope to a dark and disastrous time for this employee.

Second Chances

Sometimes, part of building people up in order to create a positive company culture means giving them second chances. The following story about Alberto is a perfect illustration of this.

Alberto was in his early twenties with limited experience in our industry (sounds like someone else I know), when we hired him to work at one of our locations. He was given the job of installing and repairing tires. Within days it was evident that he would be a positive presence in the shop. He learned very quickly and worked like a champ. He had a lot of really great skills, including a dependable and consistent work ethic. He was also bilingual in both Spanish and English, and he always had a big smile on his face. It was very clear that Alberto was going to become a great leader: He had very natural leadership abilities. When things were slow, he grabbed a broom and swept the shop floor. No one asked him to do this, and he did not make a big deal about it; he just did it. This influenced others to follow his lead.

A month or so after being hired, Alberto became the foreman of the tire technicians and was well respected by the team. He kept his work area clean and well organized. He was anxious to learn more skills and got trained on changing oil and other fluids. Alberto did not just change oil; he studied the nuances of the different oils, revamping the inventory stocking system. I had total and complete confidence in his ability to order fluid and filter inventory based on what sizes and products we would need. At the time, our oil-change hoist was located outside our small building, and he worked out there in 100-degree heat in the summer and on 20-degree days during the winter, without complaining.

Alberto wanted to learn sales, so we started to train him for this. Then he made a mistake: a big mistake. He was going through a tough time financially, with an unexpected child being born, and he was desperate to pay some bills. After taking a set of tires off a customer's car that still had some decent tread, he made a deal with a different customer to sell the used tires to them for cash. The plan was to sneak the used tires into his vehicle and then meet the customer in the grocery store parking lot down the street and make the exchange. Because our shop does not track used tires as closely as new tire inventory, he could sell the tires and keep the cash, and it would be difficult for anyone to find out about it. Fortunately for me (and him), someone saw him and reported it.

The next day, I calmly confronted Alberto and asked him about the planned exchange. He looked at the ground, his smile quickly faded, and he admitted to stealing the tires. It was clear that he was distraught. He apologized profusely and gave me the money, promising it would never happen again. I said, "Alberto, this breaks my heart. It is really disappointing that you feel the need to steal from the company. If you were that desperate for money, why didn't you tell me? I know you are an amazing person. You are better than this, and you will accomplish great things, but you will ruin it all if you go down this path." Then I said, "Stealing is a serious error that I cannot tolerate. We really need you here, but if it happens again, in the slightest degree, your employment will be terminated and I could press criminal charges." He said he agreed and understood. Not tearing Alberto down did not mean there was no accountability expected of him. People can still be held accountable in a respectful way when their actions are unacceptable.

Alberto continued to get trained in sales, and he got better and better, as was his custom. A few months later, I could not believe what happened. He was such a put-together person that I was sure he would learn his lesson and move up the ranks as a great member of our team. However, one of the other employees saw him throw a case of motor oil (12 quarts) over the fence. The Volkswagen he drove took expensive oil, and even though employees can buy this oil at cost, he decided to save some money by stealing it. After throwing the box over the fence, he drove his car to that spot and put the box in his car. It was not smart. The security cameras showed him taking the oil very clearly, and he was busted.

I pulled him into my office and said, "I saw on the cameras that you took the oil." Again, he looked down, put his head in his hands, and said, "So I'm gone, right?" I said, "Yes." There was no yelling, no belittling, no berating. He knew the expectation, and he knew the consequence. I was so angry, even though I didn't show it. I was mad that a great person with so much to offer the world was going to throw it all away over $50 worth of oil. He thanked me for the opportunity to work there and for all that he had learned and then left. My hope for him as he went on his way was that he would figure things out one day.

Fast-forward nine years: In 2018, Kory and I bought an existing tire store. The outgoing owner was telling me about his team and was so thrilled with a particular salesperson who was one of the best he had ever worked with. He said, "Alberto is amazing. You're going to love him." I had not seen or heard from Alberto since the day he left my store, but I wondered if maybe it could be the same person.

Alberto

When we bought the business, I sat down with each employee and was ecstatic to see Alberto again after so many years. He looked great, smiling and positive, like the Alberto I knew. He started by apologizing, and I told him there was no need and that I was excited to work with him again. Then he thanked me for firing him and holding him accountable for what he had done. He said that at first he had been mad at me after all the hard work he did for our company, and he vowed never to work in a tire store again. But then he said that as some time passed, this incident became the wake-up call he needed. He saw that because I had expressed my high expectations for him and told him that losing him would affect our company and that we needed him, he realized it was he who had let us down.

After bouncing around a few jobs, he knew he had skills that worked well in a tire store, so he found work in the industry again and made a decision to change his life for the better. Alberto made commitments to himself that he was going to be a good citizen and a good father to his daughter. The job he took was great, and they trained him well. With time, he met a wonderful woman and got married. She introduced him to religion, and he enjoyed it and embraced it. His skills at work got better quickly, and his income went up.

When we were reunited, Alberto seemed like a new person compared to the one who left my store in 2009, and he is truly awesome. He had always been a great person; he just needed to take a detour for a little while to see that fact for himself: that he had built a great foundation for himself and that the positive person he was and the skills he possessed were needed in the industry. Alberto learned that to be needed and to feel needed is a powerful force for good that inspires and motivates a person to change, to become all that they can be, and to help build up others in the process.

Building people up includes second chances and sometimes third chances. It includes forgiving and moving forward when the person has proven their desire to build the organization in a positive and constructive way. Alberto is now one of our most successful and productive salespeople, and he is now building up others in the company, along with the company itself. I have the chance to work with Alberto from time to time and am very grateful for that opportunity.

Principles of Leadership That Build Strong Organizations

In addition to the guidelines I shared earlier in this chapter on believing in people and not expecting perfection in your efforts to build them up, I now want to share a few more principles that have helped guide me and my leadership style in my efforts to create a strong company culture that values the people within it. These principles can further help you in your efforts to lead in a way that promotes growth and progression; they have shaped how I view people, how I treat them, and how I communicate my need for them. I hope they will do the same for you.

Instill a Deep Sense of Purpose

My goal is to build an organization of people who care deeply about performing their job at a very high level, who value others, and who want to be successful (we will explore this idea further in chapter 3: Find People Who Enjoy Work). I have found this is most effective when our organization has a purpose or vision for the way we want to do business that is based on more than just making money and becoming highly financially successful.

In some company cultures, the only thing that matters is results at any cost. Many organizations are driven by the need to publicly show, in dollars and cents, that they are better than everyone else. I disagree with this philosophy. If I am at the top, how did I get there? Did I steamroll other people, or did I lift others up with me along the way?

A rise to the top of what people consider success, fame, fortune, and recognition—if built on the backs of others in a mood of dominance and self-absorption—is abject failure. If I am given awards, how did I get them? Who has lifted me and helped me along the way?

I have heard people say they are "self-made." I am not sure how that is possible. The successful people I know do not exist in a vacuum: They have at least one person who helped them. I have launched many companies and have figured out how to grow them into successful businesses, but I definitely did not do all that by myself. It happened largely because many people showed love to me along the way. It started with my parents, who lovingly taught me to work and made education a priority. Then my sister, Kollette, partnered with me to make scrapbooking products and taught me—through her amazing example of perseverance and determination—many things I used later in the Big O Tires franchise venture. Kory took a chance on me by partnering with me even though I lacked experience. And there are many other mentors who have taken the time to talk me through strategies and ideas over the years (like Annette at my accounting job I mentioned earlier in this chapter). They have not done this to get something back monetarily; they have done it because they genuinely care about me, my family, and my success. That's all based on love, and it has been critical to my growth as a person and to the success of my organization. Instilling this love as the foundation of your company and making it the deep sense of purpose and intention which lies at the core of all you do is critical for your personal and organizational success.

I once worked closely with a colleague who trained corporate executives all over the world. The training consisted partly of identifying what each executive felt were the most important aspects of their life. Inevitably, they would name certain people (family, friends, and co-workers) as the most significant things in their life. Then the trainer asked the corporate leaders to determine how much time and focus they placed on chasing wealth versus how much time they focused on people. For many of them, the experience led to the stark realization that they had spent their career doing exactly the opposite of what they truly valued. My colleague explained that in these trainings he witnessed many powerful corporate leaders break down in tears as they realized they had created wealth at a great cost: the cost of destroying their relationships with others.

Leaders should not just be builders of businesses or builders of wealth—loads of entrepreneurs have figured out how to do that—they should also be *builders of other people.*

True greatness is based on how well you make those around you feel that they matter, and whether they know they are valued by you. I can guarantee that the organizations built on principles of hard work, ethics, moral values, and the importance of people will rise to the top and stay there. Leaders set on wealth creation at the expense of everyone else end up with an empty shell of acclaim and achievement. At some point, it dawns on them that the money and celebrity they acquired was not worth the people they trampled on to get it. I believe that true success in life is created while lifting and believing in others, and that financial accomplishment will likely accompany it.

Rules and Expectations Should Be Used to Help Others Grow, Not Just to Punish Them

When something goes wrong, when expectations are not met, when someone makes a mistake, or when flaws come to the surface, are your responses to these problems appropriate? Or are they like the manager I mentioned earlier, who came unglued when our young driver did not come back from a delivery on time? Rules should be reasonable, and when expectations are not met, they should not be used as a club with which to beat people over the head. Instead, they should be used to help you work with employees in a positive way that encourages growth *and* accountability.

I really believe that people are great. Even when a person makes a bad mistake, I believe in redemption. I believe they can recognize their faults, try to fix them, and become better—if they have that desire. I always want to give people the opportunity to fix their mistakes and move forward with a chance at redemption.

Even though I believe in redemption, there absolutely has to be accountability as well. Redemption is not allowing people to make the same mistake over and over without repercussions. Love is not looking the other way and letting someone get away with inappropriate behavior. The following are a few ways to hold people accountable while still valuing and believing in them:

People Must Understand Expectations before Any Consequences Can Be Doled Out

Expecting your people to follow the rules requires that they know the expectation before any consequence can be given. It is unjust to hold someone accountable for something they do not fully understand. My teenage daughter has recently decided to hang out with her friends later than I would like! One night, she was still out at midnight and I was tired and angry that she wasn't yet home. I said to my wife, Crystal, "Why is she out so late!? She's in trouble. I'm taking her phone for a week!" My wife then said, "Well, what time did you ask her to be home?" I replied, "We didn't talk about it. What did you tell her?" Crystal said that she hadn't talked with our daughter about it either. I knew then that I was stuck. The easy cop-out would be to say that our daughter should know better or that it's common sense to be home by midnight, but that would be a lie. Just like my wife and I are responsible (as the leaders of our family) to make sure our daughter understands the expectations, business leaders and organizational heads are responsible for making sure expectations are communicated clearly to team members.

People Must Understand the Consequences for Falling Short of an Expectation

In addition to clearly communicating expectations, leaders must also clarify the consequence for falling short of them. Remember what happened when Alberto stole oil from the store? He knew his employment would be terminated because the expectation and the consequence had been clearly established before he made the mistake. We have a firm and well-established policy for holding associates accountable in our stores, including a set number of verbal warnings, written warnings, suspensions without pay, and grounds for termination. There are few exceptions to this escalation of consequences, including stealing, violence, and discrimination. With stealing (as evidenced in Alberto's case), I gave him one chance at redemption. Violence and discrimination, on the other hand, do not get the benefit of multiple warnings.

People Must Understand the Reward for Exceeding Expectations

Finally, when expectations are exceeded, people ought to be rewarded; this helps them feel valued and needed. Make sure they understand that there will be a reward. A basic paycheck is not a reward. Rewards should go above and beyond a paycheck. I try to avoid the temptation to be cheap and say that people should just be motivated to do better because it is part of their job. If you want to build your team up and help them grow and progress so they can be part of helping the company grow and progress, set up expectations within your organization that exceptional behavior will be rewarded.

Personally, I enjoy the rewards of growing my organization if I work harder and smarter, including financial gains, the ability to travel and enjoy the outdoors, and more flexibility to spend time with my family. People are motivated by different rewards, so I try to figure out what motivates each person. Some are motivated by financial rewards; others like more vacation days or other perks. It is my job to put incentives in place to encourage great behavior. These incentives include commissions or bonuses for finding opportunities for add-on sales, reaching safety goals, and avoiding customer service complaints.

When people understand very clearly what is expected, they know exactly what will happen when they fall short or when they nail it. Everyone is on the same page, and it makes future conversations about performance (whether good or bad) fairly easy.

Be Willing to Hear What Others Think of You

When I have the guts, I ask team members to share very honestly what they think of how I am doing. Hopefully, I have created an environment where people are not afraid of me, and they will speak candidly. One way to do this is to ask, "What are three things you would do differently if you were in my position?" I do not always agree with all three of their suggestions, but I usually find that at least one is a really great idea that I can use to improve myself as an organizational head. I love letting the person know that what they said mattered to me and has some value, so I work to make that change, and it's rewarding to see how they feel when they notice.

Be Grateful and Express It

Gratitude goes a long way toward helping people feel needed and valued. Although I am extremely grateful for the amazing people I get to work with, I do a terrible job of verbally expressing it, which is something I am working to change. When I do remember and take the time to show my thanks, the impact is obvious and immediate. Showing appreciation builds confidence in your team members and makes them feel like the work they are doing matters. Don't assume that the paycheck you are giving them is enough, as I mentioned earlier. Along with the money, tell them how their efforts make a difference. You will be amazed at how much harder your team will work and how much more innovative and creative they will become. As I said, a little gratitude goes a long way.

Although verbally expressing appreciation is not my strength, I do try to show gratitude in other ways. Every summer, we close the stores for a day and go to an amusement or water park with our families. Our associates love getting away from the business and having the chance to get to know each other's families. When I have shared this tradition with other franchisees, they have asked how we can possibly afford to give up a day's worth of sales just to go play, but I tell them we usually have higher than normal sales the day after the event. Yes, we lose some sales and it costs money to take everyone and their families to an amusement park, but I look at it as an important investment in our team that's worth the money.

During the holidays at the end of the year, we also rent out a large movie theater and watch a family-friendly film together. If it has been a good year, we budget for toys and gifts for the kids, and it is always a big hit. These simple events help create a culture of optimism, light, and energy. And it is not uncommon for our associates to get together in small groups after work to go to dinner, play sports, or just hang out.

At this point, you might be picturing my business as a tire store utopia, with endless high-fives and employees singing "Kumbaya." I hope you will get that picture right out of your head, and quickly. I will be the first to admit that I often fall short of my own platitudes, and we mess things up sometimes. When things do go wrong—when I make a mistake, lose my temper, or judge someone too harshly or without good evidence—I can immediately see the difference in the energy of the organization. It is then that I notice no one is "feeling the love." When the team is not feeling the love, it means we likely aren't going to sell as much and will lose profits. While the motivation to treat people well should not just be about bringing in those profits hand over fist, a team that feels built up, needed, and valued is abso-lutely going to affect the bottom line, which ultimately ensures bene-fits having to do with more than just money. A strong, hard-working, *loving* team makes all the difference.

So, how has building a strong foundation with a culture where people feel needed and valued affected our bottom line? As I mentioned in chapter 1, after Jose Cordova taught me what I now call the "Mango Principle" about the importance of creating connections, and as we brought on more people with light and positive energy, our sales and productivity grew quickly. In 2010, when I told the team at the 9th South store we would someday get back to the $6 million in sales the previous owner had achieved in 2006, we had just hit $4.9 million in sales. By 2017, we were able to build a new 13-bay building next to the old shop, and sales shot up to $6.8 million, shattering the previous record. I believe achieving that milestone would not have been possible without the good people I worked with to make it happen. There is no way that we could have reached that level of success without their contributions.

As much as my team has needed the jobs they hold in our various stores, I have needed all the valuable skills, experience, and light they have given to our organization. As I have worked to build my team members up, their response to my positive expectations of them has, in turn, built up our company.

If you are struggling to grow your business, I encourage you to consider where you can improve in making your team members feel more needed and valued. In the next chapter, we will explore the power and productivity you can bring to your venture when you surround yourself with people who enjoy work (which means, in part, avoiding the temptation to hire cheap labor).

3

Find People Who Enjoy Work

"Remember that you are needed. There is at least one important work to be done that will not be done unless you do it."

—Charles L. Allen

My schoolteacher parents did not just hand out money to us kids. Our family always had the essentials covered, like nourishing home-cooked meals (fish sticks and green beans), Toughskins jeans, and a hand-me-down baseball glove. But I was very aware as a child that there wasn't much extra to go around. So at a young age, I began to be very motivated to earn money and was always on the lookout for jobs I could do and ways to make a few bucks. Early on, I learned the very important lesson that there are endless inventive ways to earn money, and this filled me with a certain kind of energy to try to figure out how to get jobs and do them more effectively than others. Work, for me, somehow became fun.

Realizing that work can be enjoyable didn't come all at once; I had to learn that along the way as I did some pretty disagreeable jobs initially (the cherry harvest comes to mind that I mentioned in the last chapter) and the job I had working for my dad at age eight, pulling dandelions in the yard: my first reliable source of income.

I grew up on a half-acre in northern Utah, and my dad was proud of his beautiful lawn and garden. There were daffodils, tulips, and marigolds (the seeds of which we would harvest and replant the next year), and roses that Dad would cut and place in a vase in the kitchen for my mom throughout the summer. With those beautiful flowers also came dandelions.

The yard took an enormous amount of work, and Dad spent many hours every Saturday out there. Hearing my bedroom light click on and him roaring, "Let's go! Up and at 'em!" was not a welcome sound on Saturday mornings. He handed me a "toad-stabber" (forked hand-weeder) and said he'd give me a nickel for each dandelion I pulled— with the root attached. It was hot and it was hard, but one summer I did manage to earn $32. With the money came a sense of satisfaction in actually sticking with something I didn't feel all too excited about doing.

Observing others, I soon learned there were more and better ways to make money than just pulling weeds in our yard. My first real business "venture" began as a newspaper and pop can recycling operation with my older brother, Kamron. We asked neighbors for their soda cans and their used copies of the *Ogden Standard-Examiner* and collected them in an old, rusty wagon. Then we bundled the papers and sold them and the pop cans to the recycler in downtown Ogden, Utah. Doing this earned us each between $8 and $12 a week, and through this little venture I figured out how to talk to people and get customers. I realized I loved the process and loved figuring out how to make money, so I started looking for ways to sell things door-to-door.

One year, the elementary school asked us students to sell raffle tickets to raise money to build a new gymnasium. When the bell rang, I bolted out of the school doors and ran up the half-mile hill toward my home, going door to door, covering the entire neighborhood and selling a ton of tickets before anyone else had even thought about heading out to work the streets. Later that evening, I watched a group of about ten kids going together from house to house, trying to peddle tickets. I could tell they weren't selling any, and I knew it was because no one was going to buy from a group since they would have to purchase one ticket from each child, *and* (more importantly) because those people had already bought from me! That knowledge was incredibly satisfying. I think I got a prize for being the top salesperson at the school, though I didn't make any money. To me it didn't matter. Coming to the realization that the challenge of work can be enjoyable was part of the reward for me.

Another time, Kamron was selling chocolate bars for a fundraiser of some kind, and I wanted in on the action. As a third-grader, I went to the house of the man who was a distributor for the chocolate company and worked out a deal with him. I asked him if I could sell his chocolate and keep some of the money for myself. He told me I could keep half. With a cardboard box of chocolate bars in hand, I hit the road and began selling $1 and $2 bars. I did a test to see if I could make more money selling $1 bars or $2 bars and found I could sell more than double of the $1 candy, so I made more money that way. That's because people will spend $1 on anything.

One Saturday, my goal was to sell two 15-count boxes of bars, which would bring me $15 profit for just a few hours of work; it was good money for me. On one of these Saturdays, a friend asked if he could tag along, but he didn't last very long because he said I walked too fast. Sometimes I couldn't resist jogging from house to house; I had little patience for walking and the time wasted between homes. I think I got some extra sales because people felt bad when I showed up sweating and red-faced!

There were a variety of other things I pitched to my neighbors over the years. I sold magazine subscriptions, gift wrap, and pizzas. Can you imagine having to live near me!? People would, no doubt, cringe when they saw me coming. Sometimes I would give them a break by having my dad drop me off at neighborhoods farther away. Without a cell phone (in those days), it was always a long walk home but definitely worth it.

By the time I entered college, I had worked in a variety of different jobs and launched a bunch of money-making ventures. Now I needed real money to pay tuition at Brigham Young University, where I was attending. It was 1999, and the world was soon "going to end," or so everyone said as Y2K approached and all computers were supposedly going to stop functioning. Utility grids would go down, banking data would be lost, and the world would be thrown into utter chaos.

So to earn more money for college, I got a job selling emergency kits to take advantage of the situation. The bright yellow kit contained a butane lantern, stove, and space heater. The company gave me little support, so I had to figure out how to sell the kits on my own. I started by going door-to-door (it did not go well), then got a booth at county fairs (it went very well), and finally rented a kiosk in a mall for a month (it went okay, but I hated being tied to that kiosk all day!). I made enough money to get through another semester of college, and the world didn't collapse, which was a bonus.

When the world didn't end, Kory hired me to work at his employer, BFI Waste Services, as a residential garbage can delivery and repair boy. After picking up broken or unused garbage cans, I cleaned them up and repaired them. It was not glamorous, and it was stinky, but I thought of some cool ways to improve the simple system I had to work with and even did some things to increase business.

The new, fast-growing town of Eagle Mountain west of Utah Lake did not have a garbage contract with any single company. Each resident had to sign up for their own service, and they could choose from a couple of different waste collection vendors. There was a ton of new home construction going on, so I thought of a way to get a lot of the new residents signed up. I met with the three biggest building contractors out there and asked them if they would include a BFI Waste contract and subscription instructions with each resident's welcome packet when they moved into their new home. All three agreed to do so in exchange for one free garbage can and service at their model home. We signed up hundreds of new residents with the help of the building contractors, and the free service we provided only cost the company $10 a month.

I feel that all these experiences in my youth were very instrumental in helping me build the businesses that I operate today. I suppose much of the reason why I felt I could take on the Big O Tires franchise in Salt Lake City at just 28 years old was because of the confidence I acquired as a kid learning how to enjoy work and figuring out how to solve problems and do things better. Although I was grossly unprepared to run an automotive repair shop and had to learn some very costly lessons—the hard way—I think my love of hard work and the satisfaction I find in doing a job well made up for a lot of my poor decisions early on. Of course, our company's success and positive business culture cannot be attributed to my efforts alone; a major part of our success has come because I look for people who have this love for work when I recruit and hire. As I have been trying to convey throughout this book, the people you surround yourself with are very important: people who enjoy work and want to make a difference.

Some of the tasks in my business are not considered extremely enjoyable by many people: things such as working on a freezing cold, soaking wet tire for instance. But people who enjoy work are more likely to get satisfaction from performing these types of difficult tasks. Whatever the work, I have learned that I benefit the most when I hire individuals who are willing to approach their work with the same energy I do.

> Organizational success has only come to me as I have valued people who are filled with light (as I outlined in chapter 1), enthusiastic about their work, willing to team up with me to ensure the collective success of everyone in the organization, and excited about accomplishing something that matters.

Over the next few pages, I want to outline some of the things that have helped me attract and retain these types of people and how you can discern what kind of team player a potential hire will be based on a few key characteristics that are common among those who find real satisfaction in their work and in helping others find satisfaction in theirs.

Finding People Who Love to Work

Most of the people on our team at the tire stores work long, hard hours: at least a ten-hour day, and they are on their feet the entire time. It is taxing physically and mentally, so we have to make sure we employ those people who have what it takes to do this kind of work.

When we hire someone new, we don't necessarily judge them too much on the specific skill they will need to perform the job or how much they still have to learn about their work. Instead, we look for the following characteristics to assess their attitude toward work and their willingness to be a team player who can bring positive energy to our shops:

- Do they jump in and try?
- Do they ask questions?
- Do they find something to do during down time, even if it is very simple?

Jumping In

There are two main ways that new hires can learn our systems and processes. We can teach them certain principles, or they can jump in on their own and learn from trial and error. Learning often takes place through a combination of both: we teach some basics, and then the employee needs to jump in and give it a try. You can tell a lot about a person by how willing they are to attempt new things, even when they don't know what in the heck they're doing. People who are willing to take those kinds of risks tend to be those who love to learn. I have found that anyone who loves to learn also tends to enjoy the work they do.

My brother-in-law Jason Hall who I quoted at the end of chapter 1, is an excellent example of someone who is willing to jump in and try, even when things are *extremely* difficult.

As a quadriplegic who was paralyzed from the chest down, Jason had been told he would never live away from home, never attend college, never marry, and never provide for himself or a family. But Jason was no quitter and overcame all of these limitations. He spoke about his first day of work at a professional job, where he had to use his tenacious drive and determination to jump into something that was truly more than he thought he could handle at the time:

> *The first day I started selling life insurance at Mutual of New York, I went into the office to learn side-by-side from my highly successful manager, Chuck.*
>
> *Chuck told me to bring in a list of 100 names, people who knew me, leads I could call that might be interested in buying life insurance. I was ready.*
>
> *But Chuck forgot it was my first day.*
>
> *He already had a full day of appointments. Apologizing, he cleared off his desk and invited me to move into his spot. He placed the phone in front of me, handed me his calendar and said, "Take out your list of 100 people and start calling."*
>
> *He left me alone with my list, the phone, and an almost debilitating fear. I had no idea how to sell insurance, no idea how to convince people to meet with me. Sitting there all by myself, my first-day excitement and confidence evaporated. In an instant, I wasn't even sure I wanted to do this anymore.*
>
> *I stared at the phone as the sweat began to form on my brow and my heart rate increased. Then a photo on Chuck's*

desk caught my eye. It was a picture of his family in front of their beautiful home. That picture represented everything I wanted in my life, every reason I had pursued this career in the first place. That picture was my purpose. I simply wanted to take care of my family. I looked at that phone again and thought, "If I want to get what's in that picture, I have to go through this phone."

I took a deep breath, picked up the receiver, and punched in the number of the first person on my list. As I learned that day and many hard days afterward, true purpose inspires devoted action.

Many insurance agents work years to make it to a Million Dollar Round Table—a premier association of financial professionals—but Jason did it in just two months, his first year in the business, establishing himself as part of the top six percent of those in his profession. He reached this level of success because of his willingness to jump in, even when he didn't know what he was doing. People like Jason are the kind you want to hire in your business: individuals who aren't afraid to try.

Being willing to try, which often means making mistakes, should not be punished by team leaders and organizational heads. Valuing people so you can attract and keep those who enjoy their work and can help build your business means not expecting perfection right off the bat. Berating people who do jump in and try is a great way to stunt the growth of your organization and to confound all the other people who work with you and around you. Instead of helping people feel empowered and more willing to go the distance for you, it makes people draw back, constantly second guess their decisions, and be fearful of thinking outside the box and coming up with creative solutions to everyday problems. No one wants to look "stupid" or be thought of as "less than," so they will hold back in an environment where leadership is too critical. This does nothing to create a positive company culture, and I believe it ultimately affects the bottom line.

I have seen our own managers scold brand-new people for making mistakes. But almost all of the errors are things that the new worker would not know or understand. Inevitably, the new hire will say, "I'm sorry, I didn't know." Also inevitably, the manager will say, "You should have known—it's common sense!" We get so used to our own systems and processes that these things start to feel innate. We forget that we once did not have the knowledge we now possess, and we assume that everyone knows certain things that we have learned over time. To us, these things are extremely basic and so fundamental that obviously everyone would know them.

But even though (in an auto repair shop in my case) a new worker on their first day is going to break a valve stem or damage a tool, we must value—very highly—someone's desire to jump in and try, despite all the ways they will mess up in the beginning. Those early mistakes can be costly, but I believe that someone who has a desire to learn and who takes the initiative to try is someone who loves work, and that quality is worth more than the cost of their mistakes. And if they love work and have a purpose, they will learn to be a great asset over time.

If you are a parent, I'm sure your kids have humbled you to the core as they have reminded you, from time to time, that it is ridic-ulous for you to expect them to know the same amount of things you do, even if you consider those things to be fundamentally basic.

Hopefully, we cut our children slack in this regard, keeping in mind that they are new here on the earth and are just learning. Of course, we don't want to treat new hires as children, but we can approach their level of knowledge in the same way we do with kids: having realistic expectations of them and recognizing their progress in the learning process. Good parents want their children to grow up to be capable, confident risk-takers who can navigate their way around the world. If we want our employees to become powerfully proficient in the jobs they do, we must treat them as if we believe they are capable of meeting our expectations. When we do so, everyone wins. Team members love coming to work and performing at their best, and this in turn builds the organization. The cycle repeats itself over and over as more positive energy is expended in making sure the mutual success of everyone is assured.

We recently hired someone who is not afraid to jump in and try, even though he is new at the job. Joel is about 20 years old and fresh out of auto mechanic trade school. Although he has zero workplace experience, he is excited to be employed as a trained mechanic in our shop.

On his first day, I met him and asked, "Do you have a toolbox?" He sheepishly exclaimed, "Yep!" and pointed at a beat-up cardboard box with a handful of tools haphazardly thrown into it. I chuckled to myself. I have never seen a mechanic bring his tools in a cardboard box. In our world, that takes guts. He is young, he has no money . . . and he is hungry. He knows he lacks the proper equipment but came ready to jump in and make things happen anyway, the best he could.

Later that day, at lunch time, another employee noticed that Joel didn't eat lunch and asked him if he had any food. When Joel said he didn't, his co-worker shared some of his. I asked Joel if he had money for food, and he said no but that his brother might have some instant ramen he could eat until payday. I offered to help him with some food, but he graciously declined and said he was fine. I offered to lend him money for tools and a toolbox, but he told me he didn't want to start out at his first job in debt and preferred to save up for those things. Joel is hungry. Literally.

A few mornings later, I noticed that Joel arrived at work walking from the nearby light-rail train station. Traveling to work via public transportation is not super common in our area, and all of our other employees drive cars to work. There is not a lot of traffic, we have plenty of parking, and public transportation often doubles the commute time. I asked Joel why he preferred the train. He said that his car wasn't running because it needed a $400 part. Then he quickly

Joel

added that it was fine to take the train for now; he didn't mind the longer commute, and that he was saving up to fix his car.

Joel is the perfect example of a person who enjoys work. On his first day, with limited tools, he jumped in and did his best without whining or complaining. His hunger and desire to grow and learn despite his age, experiences, and resources has been inspiring to his co-workers, and they have shared tools and helped him become part of a team of people who are positive and filled with light.

Asking Questions

Many new employees are concerned that they will be annoying or look dumb if they ask questions. It is our job to make sure we reassure them that we want them to ask questions, we expect there to be many questions, and it is not a bother to us when they make inquiries about how to do their job. Even with that initial reassurance, we might need to repeat this over and over again to remind them.

The manager of one of our stores was annoyed by a new, young sales associate. I'll call him Joe. Joe was eloquent, dependable, and had a good track record of reliability at his other jobs. Without knowing him well, it seemed he was someone who liked to work. After some initial instruction to simply observe the other salespeople, Joe got distracted. He was on his cell phone and walking around without any kind of focus or attention to anyone or anything. After a few days of this, his manager called me and said that Joe was horrible, he was lazy, and he was not going to work out.

I drove out to that location to meet with Joe. I asked him what he had learned during his first three days. He was concerned because he was not learning or progressing, and he had left other work because he really thought this would be a good career move for him and his young family. I liked that he had a desire to succeed at his job and that he had a purpose. While sitting in the little office, I told him that we look for people who are willing to jump in and give it a try. I asked him why he wasn't learning. He said that everyone was so busy he didn't want to bother them with questions. He also felt that when he did ask questions, the other workers brushed him off as an annoyance, and he did not want to bother them, so he stopped asking.

I then had a quick huddle with Joe and the manager. I said, "Joe is new. I believe in Joe, and I believe he can be a great asset to our company. He has a job requirement to put away his phone and ask a question at least every five minutes. Let the other members of the team know that he has an assignment from me to bother them with questions all day."

Joe fulfilled his assignment. It turns out that he loves to work, and he just needed permission to ask all the questions required to learn his job and jump in, even though he would make mistakes. Within another week, he was contributing considerably to our team and is now a great asset to our company.

Doing Something When There Seems to Be Nothing to Do

This quality is easy to spot. When a person looks for something to do when there is nothing to do, you know you have someone who loves work.

A friend of mine has a neighbor named Alex. Alex is a professional with multiple college degrees; he is very intelligent and hardworking. As a former employee of The Church of Jesus Christ of Latter-day Saints, he successfully helped oversee church operations in a large area of South America. He is widely respected for his intellect and abilities. What might surprise you, however, is that Alex currently spends his working hours at a shop where he cleans up trash, scrubs grimy floors, and cleans bathrooms.

You see, Alex is a refugee from Venezuela. He and his family made their way to our country a couple of years ago to escape the tyranny of socialist dictators. Even with his education and job, his family was starving. Even with a steady paycheck, there was no food to buy. While he worked through the legal process of obtaining political asylum and a work visa, he was sponsored by my friend, who supported Alex and his family as they learned a new language, culture, and everything else they would need to know to live and work in the U.S.

I have met Alex a couple of times, and he has always stood out to me because he continually has a smile on his face—as he's sweeping the floor at the shop where he was finally able to get a job. Even though he is doing work that is well beneath his education and intellectual abilities, this does not seem to bother Alex. He is a relentless, happy worker, always grateful, always seeing what needs to be done and doing it without being asked. Alex is a self-directed guy who can take initiative on his own, a person that any organization would be fortunate to have on their team no matter what assignment was given to him.

Since learning how important it is to value people and to attract and retain those who can bring a positive energy into my organization, I have made it a priority to hire people like Alex and Robbie Carter (the top salesperson at the 9th South store who is now that location's manager). Robbie loves to work, and it is easy to see that because of the way he approaches his job. He has an infectious energy, as I noted in chapter 1; as a challenge to himself, he often creates games to make work more fun and interesting.

One day, during a slow part of the afternoon, a red Toyota Camry pulled into a parking space in front of our store. Robbie said, "I bet you I can sell this guy tires in 30 seconds or less." We took the bet. As the man walked toward the front door, Robbie went outside and asked him how he could help. The man said, "I need a price on tires." Robbie replied, "Five hundred dollars—and I can pull it in right now." The man handed Robbie his keys and came inside while Robbie drove his Toyota into the bay. No more than 30 seconds had passed from the time the customer got out of his car to when his car was in the shop getting new tires.

Now of course we typically train our people to discuss different tire options, see what other services a customer might need, and get all of their information before we try to make a sale. Those things can be an effective part of the service process, but those things can also bog us down. While the shoot-from-the-hip pricing strategy Robbie took is generally not the most effective, in this case, his enthusiastic, no-fuss approach to a sale energized our team.

Afterward, Robbie of course got the customer's information and we did a vehicle inspection, where he was then able to sell the customer an alignment and new brakes. I love that Robbie broke protocol at that moment and took the initiative needed to not only sell the man a new set of tires but provide two other needed services as well. His energy and love for the work he does rubs off on others and inspires them to want to approach their job with more enthusiasm. Having people like Robbie in our organization makes all the difference.

Avoid the Temptation of Cheap Labor

Another way to ensure that you attract people who enjoy work is to avoid cheap labor. As Warren Buffet has said, "Price is what you pay. Value is what you get." I had to learn this the hard way when I hired cheap labor in order to "save on payroll" in the early, disastrous days at the 9th South store. I found that this was no way to attract the kind of people who are self-motivated achievers interested in helping me grow and strengthen my business.

When I go to my favorite fast-food restaurant chain, In-N-Out Burger, my experience is always amazing and always the same. In the drive-thru, after giving my usual order of a "Double-Double" (double patty, double cheese) and a vanilla shake, the worker kindly repeats the order back to me to verify they have it correct. "Kindly" is actually an understatement. I can hear her bright smile and joyous expression through the intercom. With an average line of 20 cars that snake around the building all day long, I have to wonder where she gets the pep and the endless supply of positive energy to serve me like this.

When I get to the window, another boisterous soul greets me and again repeats my order to verify its accuracy. Before handing me the food, he smiles and energetically asks me if I will be dining in my car and if I will need a placemat for my lap. As he verifies the order one more time, I feel like royalty.

Burger bag in hand, the employee gives me the shake with a straw inserted and a couple inches of paper wrapper left on the top of the straw. The next time I go to In-N-Out, I'll hear a different voice at the drive-up, but I'll still get the same pep and friendly service. The food will still be great (it's consistently good, and to me, it's the best burger for the price, anywhere) and I will wait in a long line to eat there.

So how does In-N-Out do it?

This popular restaurant chain is a West Coast phenomenon. Each location has a massive crew of well-paid, well-trained workers to create the ultimate fast-food experience. Starting wages are much higher than what the average fast-food worker is usually paid in this market. Managers make up to $160,000 per year but are not required to have a high school diploma, much less a college degree, and many of them make more money than college-trained engineers, accountants, and developers.

Denny Warnick, executive vice president and chief operating officer of In-N-Out, explains why they pay their employees so well: "Harry and Esther Snyder founded In-N-Out Burger in 1948 upon the strong values of . . . providing the very friendliest service to our customers. From the beginning, the Snyders treated associates like family, realizing that we're only able to meet our high standards with exceptional [people] who are dedicated to making that happen."

Warnick continues, noting that paying higher wages "is one important way to make our associates feel great about working at In-N-Out. It's helpful in creating an upbeat and customer-focused atmosphere, with relatively low turnover, which leads to more experienced teams working our restaurants." He also notes that paying top wages is a way to thank their employees for the incredible job they do.

From my early mistakes at the 9th South store when I let some of the top salespeople go in order to save money, I learned that Denny Warnick is absolutely right: You have to value people by paying them well if you want to attract (and keep) the kind of team players who are enthusiastic about being part of a successful enterprise. For years, I have felt bad about letting good people go because I did not understand their value. I thought I would increase profits by replacing higher priced, higher quality labor with cheap labor, and it was a lesson that stung badly.

Today, our tire stores are highly profitable *because* we pay high wages, not in spite of it. Now, I find the best people I can, and I pay what I need to for them to be excited to join our team and to maintain that level of enthusiasm as they stay loyal to our company. Thankfully we have not experienced the kind of turnover typical in the automotive repair industry because of this. People are by far our best asset.

Cheap Labor Negatively Affects the Organization at All Levels

Cheap labor usually means inexperience, and inexperience means more mistakes at every level of an organization:

Entry-Level Positions: *(In my case, installing or maintaining tires.)*
While a tire technician's job is usually considered entry-level, there are a lot of details of this lower-skill job that can have a big impact on the customer experience. If the air pressure of a tire isn't right, the vehicle can perform badly or pull to one side, or the tires could wear unevenly. If this happens, the customer is going to come back unhappy. We call this a "come-back." Come-backs slow down the operation because now we have to redo the work, which then affects the turnaround time of other waiting customers.

Inexperienced technicians also damage tires (torn beads), they break tire pressure monitoring sensors, and they use too many wheel weights to balance tires. Cheap labor isn't cheap. If not trained properly, cheap workers can be very expensive. The profitability of our shops is built on efficiency and accuracy, and mistakes and come-backs crush that profitability. A well-trained team with systems in place to check work and prevent come-backs lets us process more vehicles, which in turn increases sales.

Having said that, I am constantly on the hunt for great people, and by "great people," I'm not just talking about their level of experience or ability. Great team players, even if they are inexperienced, are those who have the same kind of energy and attitude toward work that I feel I possess, who are positive and upbeat, who enjoy work, and who want to learn and grow: people like Alex and Joel and my brother-in-law Jason who I mentioned earlier in this chapter. These people aren't afraid to jump in and ask questions, and they have the initiative to see what needs to be done and do it without being asked.

Because inexperience in entry-level jobs can be costly, when we find a new hire that possesses all the personal characteristics that can make him a valuable associate but may not yet have the skillset we will ultimately need, we pair them with a mentor. This means the new hire cannot work on their own until the mentor is willing to vouch for their ability to perform the job without significant mistakes. Because of this, we tend to carry a few more people on our payroll than most shops in our industry. However, we look at this additional labor as an absolute necessity because they are helping us continually hire and train our next leaders: leaders who will help us grow and take us to greater heights.

In addition to pairing inexperienced new workers with a mentor, we also pay higher than average wages, even for untrained people coming into entry-level positions. That's because we seek career-oriented team players. Cheap is tempting, but it is not recommended.

I encourage you to assess your entry-level workers and what you are paying them. Are they people who enjoy work and are self-motivated, enthusiastic employees who have the potential to help you grow your business? If not, perhaps it's time to rethink things. And if you have good people in these lower-level jobs, are you paying them well enough to help them stay enthusiastic about you and your organization? If not, why not? Remember, you get what you pay for.

Medium and Highly Skilled Positions: *(In my case, repairing vehicles; everything from easy part replacements to challenging diagnostics.)*

Cheap labor in medium or highly skilled positions has many of the same pitfalls as low-skilled labor. Saving money on a cheap mechanic is a bad idea. Most of the great mechanics know their value, and they make great money. To get one on my team, I know I am going to have to pay them well.

Vehicle repair technicians who make a lot of mistakes are often inexperienced, unenthusiastic about their work, or arrogant and sloppy. I am leery of technicians who tolerate a disgusting, oil-soaked work area. Generally, if they don't care about taking care of their workspace, they often don't care about taking good care of the customer's vehicle, which means to me they do not enjoy what they are doing.

Sometimes mechanics with many years of experience can lose focus on the quality of their trade and make mistakes by rushing jobs or not getting properly educated on new techniques and technologies. The people who take pride in their work, educate themselves properly, and work at learning new industry advancements cost more money. But they are worth every penny. Getting a supposedly "good deal" on a person you have hired to fill a skilled position that normally would demand top wages will likely backfire.

In my case, whether the mistakes happen from lack of experience or lack of focus, the result is the same: the dreaded come-back. Again, come-backs kill our shop. I hate them. Think of the time it takes for a customer to come back with a preventable problem. First, the customer calls the store and a worker must answer the phone and listen to the complaint. Those few minutes could have been spent working on the needs of other clients. The customer then shows up, and a worker has to stage that vehicle to be diagnosed, which takes a few more minutes. Eventually, a technician has to test-drive the vehicle, pull it into the shop, lift the car onto the hoist, and, in some cases, disassemble work that was done previously then do it again properly. All of this extra time and energy could have been avoided if the job were done correctly the first time. Usually, that requires an employee who takes pride in his or her work, loves to problem-solve, and is working to be more than just a "technician" going through the "checklist" of required items, not caring enough about what he or she does.

When we have an unenthusiastic, uncaring mechanic in our shop, we have to be prepared to spend more time fixing problems that could have been avoided. All this extra time will likely bump at least one customer to the next day, which means lost revenue today. If that happened once a day in my store, we would lose hundreds of thousands of dollars a year. Employing "cheap" labor usually turns out to be very expensive.

Sales: *(In my case, these are customer service associates, sales associates, or service writers who communicate with the customer about the needs of their vehicle.)*

In my business, cheap labor in the sales department equals low sales. It's as simple as that. I have proven it over and over again. All organizations are sales companies (as I will explain in the next chapter), and it's important to understand this about your own organization as well, no matter what product or service you provide. When I do a bad job of hiring and training sales associates, our sales go down, and I'm pretty confident that the same thing applies to your business as well. That's why I try to be obsessed with finding people who love to work; love to engage and interact with customers; are enthusiastic about our products, services, or ideals; and have a desire to sell effectively and at a very high level. Associates who understand that we are a sales company are dialed in to all aspects of the sales process and understand the following:

- The importance of building personal relationships with customers and establishing trust with them;
- The need for accurate and clear communication;
- Why it's important to keep commitments; and
- How to ask for the sale.

Cheap labor in the sales department often includes people who lack the desire to build these skills. These types of employees are usually at a job because they need a paycheck but lack the vision to go beyond the money and see how they could be a part of creating a successful organization that then brings even greater rewards.

At our stores, I have tried to train my team members to have realistic expectations about new sales associates. As I have noted in previous chapters, demanding perfection does nothing to build your company and only serves to drain the light and life out of your business. I do, however, set the expectation that sales associates should be willing to jump in and try to learn, try to progress, and push themselves to improve.

I choose to surround myself with great people who love work and love figuring out how to do their job more proficiently. Some of these people have started out at a lower wage, knowing that they will quickly be rewarded for pushing themselves to learn the necessary skills fast. However, we have generally seen more success with self-motivated sales associates who have a proven track record of an optimistic outlook and positive energy. These people usually make more money with us than they did at their previous job.

Building a strong foundation will not happen if you are trying to save on payroll. While cheap labor is tempting, don't do it. Your organization deserves the best, and it will be the best if it has the best people. Find great people—those who have light, those who are positive, those who love their work and have a desire to succeed and grow—then pay them what they're worth.

To wrap up this chapter, I want to share one final story about my dad, who taught me from an early age how to work and the value of loving that work no matter what it is. Dad was a professor of religious studies at Weber State College (now WSU), but even on busy school days he would go to work an hour early to direct traffic outside his building on campus, where vehicles often got snarled during the morning rush. Rain, sleet, or snow, he donned a bright yellow rain slicker and carried a flashlight to help out, just because the situation warranted it.

One morning when I was a kid, during a particularly bad storm, I remember asking him, "Dad, do you *have* to go direct traffic for your job?"

"Nope," he answered.

"Then why do you do it?" I asked. "Because I like it," was his response.

The significance of that response has always stayed with me.

Surrounding yourself with people who love work is a key to organizational success. If you are struggling to grow your business, I urge you to take a closer look at the attitudes of the people who are working with you and how well you pay them. If enthusiasm is waning and the tone in your organization is less than positive, perhaps now is the time to evaluate how your employees feel about their job and how you feel about them. If they need reassurance, I encourage you to hand them out lavishly. When I reassure new hires and long-time associates that they matter, that they have something to contribute to our organization, and that we need them, I am amazed at what they are willing to do to take things to the next level.

Remember, new people will make mistakes, and that's okay. I urge you to teach them that mistakes are part of the learning process and that you understand that everyone will make them. Be sure not to squelch their desire to jump in and try new things, even if this is uncomfortable for you. If your employees have this drive, don't kill it; people who aren't afraid to take risks, try new things, and problem-solve without hand-holding are becoming harder and harder to find. Let those with light shine for you.

Encourage new people to ask questions: lots and lots of questions. And look for people who want to work and have the initiative to find something to do when there seems to be nothing to do. Finding and keeping people with these qualities will help contribute to your organization's success.

When I am asked about my hobbies, I honestly can't think of any (as sad as that may sound). I love to work. I buy and sell small businesses, and when I am not working on buying and selling businesses, my hobby is thinking about buying and selling businesses (along with a fair share of my kids' games and plays mixed in). While I am pretty extreme in this aspect, a love of work has been a meaningful part of my life, and I have found success by hiring people who share that trait.

In the next chapter, we will explore how valuing the right people helps build a sales-based organization, which I alluded to earlier in this chapter as a quality that all exceptional businesses have in common. Valuing people creates a strong company culture, which in turn builds a strong sales organization that can produce tremendous benefits for everyone involved.

4

Every Organization Is a Sales Organization, Which Is Why You Need the Right People

> *"Every morning in Africa, a gazelle wakes up. It knows it must run faster than the fastest lion or it will be killed. Every morning a lion wakes up. It knows it must outrun the slowest gazelle, or it will starve to death. It doesn't matter whether you are a lion or a gazelle—when the sun comes up, you'd better be running."*
>
> —Dan Montano

J ose Cordova, the valued team member at the 9th South store who taught me the powerful Mango Principle that is the premise of this book, is married to Miriam. In late 2017—when we were on the hunt for people passionate about selling—Miriam was working at a large, competing tire store chain. Though married and working as competitors about 20 miles away from each other, Jose and Miriam were professional about their career situation and did not share competing company information with me or others.

When I mentioned to Jose that we were looking for more great sales associates, he said, "Well, there's Miriam. She's really good." I did not know her well and had no idea how she viewed the concept of selling. During an interview with her, she expressed that she would consider a change after being with the same company for 14 years; she had started there as a high school student. What stood out to me most about the interview was that she very strongly said, "I can sell." Well, everyone says that when interviewing for a sales position, but there was something about her confidence that made me believe her. We hired her, and she made an immediate impact. Miriam can, indeed, sell. She is passionate about sales and truly wants to take great care of our customers and our company.

When Miriam had been with us only a short time, Kory and I acquired another location. I knew with this acquisition that it was time for me to hire someone to help me manage all six of our stores. Even though Miriam was fairly new, I felt strongly that she should be considered for this position. She has a unique vision and mindset about selling, seeing its importance in terms of its impact on the overall success and growth of an organization.

While we actively recruit both men and women to work with us, our industry tends to attract mostly men as both technicians and salespeople; however, I believed that Miriam had the greatest number of skills out of all our associates, both men and women, and would be great for this position. Case in point: During her tenure at her former job, she had learned sales, customer service, accounts receivable, accounts payable, legal protocols, and compliance issues.

She understood training, accountability, and spreadsheets. Miriam is also ridiculously positive and has an infectious energy about her. So, I offered her the job, and she accepted the position as general manager over all our locations.

At the time, Miriam was the only woman working on the operations side of our company, yet she was fearless with a sort of mental hunger that made her passionate about breaking sales records—in every location, every year. She was determined to help make our organization grow even stronger. And with her help, we have. Revenue at all of our locations has grown and continues to do so.

Miriam

When I find associates like Miriam, who understand that we are a sales organization first and a tire/auto repair company second, I hire them and pay them well to stay with us (see chapter 3). When team members understand the principles of a good sales organization and can prove they can execute these principles through a willing, proactive outlook and the same kind of mental hunger Miriam exhibits, they make a huge difference in the way our organization progresses. *People like this are the most valuable assets in my business because sales drives everything.*

> **Successful organizations always value sales-driven people—those who are willing and able to remove limiting belief systems, are mentally hungry for greatness, and understand how to help the company stay relevant by applying sales processes and principles that bring viable profitability to the venture.**

The Principles a Sales-Driven Organization Lives By

As noted earlier in this chapter, good sales associates who are passionate about their work and are driven to succeed understand that all companies are sales organizations, regardless of what product or service they provide. If you want to grow your business and make it more profitable, it is important that you find these types of people: those who are dialed in to all aspects of the sales process and who understand the following principles (as outlined in the previous chapter):

- The importance of building personal relationships with customers and establishing trust with them;
- The need for accurate and clear communication;

- The ability to keep commitments; and
- The willingness to ask for the sale.

When I want to reform a business, I always start with the sales associates by holding them accountable to these principles. This was certainly the case with one of the tire stores in the Big O franchise that Kory and I purchased in 2018. While it was a very profitable store (the location was busy, handling between 50 and 60 cars per day), I knew right away that some aspects of the business were not being handled like a successful sales organization. The sales associates were keeping their heads above water, but they were not always communicating clearly with customers, keeping commitments, or asking for the sale. In many cases, they would work on tires without telling the customer that their car's alignment should be checked. All auto maintenance professionals understand the need to check the alignment of a vehicle, but many still do not ask the customer for that opportunity.

On the first day we owned the company, I huddled up the sales team and asked them if they could sell any more alignments. They were doing okay, making about $12,000 per month in alignment revenue (a little above average for a Big O Tires franchise) and thought they were doing all they could. To see if that were true, I installed a process for checking the alignment on more vehicles and taught them how to ask for the sale. Here's how alignment sales went the first week:

Day 1: $480
Day 2: $660
Day 3: $1,120
Day 4: $1,260

Day 5: $1,462

Day 6: $1,719

By the end of the first 30 days, we doubled alignment sales to $24,661, which added $12,000 of gross profit in one month. Under the leadership of manager Pablo Serrato, that location now regularly does over $30,000 in alignment sales every 30 days with one alignment rack, drastically higher than the industry average. Why? Because we are a sales company driven by well-trained, good-hearted sales associates who understand how to apply the sales principles noted above.

Pablo

Let's take a closer look at each of these principles:

Building Relationships of Trust with Customers

It should be very clear by now that Jose's ability to sell a ton of mangos, literally, every weekend in his family's fruit business (see the introduction) was not based on the mangos he was selling or their price: It was based on how he connected with his customers. This connection carries more weight than any other aspect of selling, but is often taken for granted, misunderstood, or forgotten altogether. Working to build a relationship of trust with our customers and giving this precedence over the product, service, price, or anything else, has been tremendously rewarding. Jan, a customer who came into our store with a brake noise on her 2014 Chevy Silverado, is a good example of what can happen when you focus on the customer first and making money second.

When Jan came to our store, she already had a quote from another shop to repair the problem with her brakes for $650. She wasn't totally happy with this quote and decided to ask us to take a look at the brakes to see why they might be making such a racket. After an inspection, our technician found a small pebble wedged in her brake system, causing the noise. He removed the rock and the noise went away; her brakes were in good shape otherwise.

After sending her on her way with no charge, Jan wrote a letter to the CEO of Big O Tires (our franchisor) about her experience with our store. It said in part, "To cap off a most appreciated, pleasant, and successful visit, they did not charge me for the repair. I wanted to make sure that Big O leadership heard directly from me about the great service that your teams are delivering on the shop floor. I am new to the area and I have located a Big O store near my home for future reference. We are Big O loyalists from here on."

Communicating Clearly with Customers

When the sales process lacks clear communication, the customer will inevitably have a bad experience. We made a big mistake one time with one particular customer, who had left his Isuzu Rodeo with us for a brake repair. We sold him brake pads and brake rotors, but during the repair it became evident that the vehicle would also need calipers. We dropped the ball on communicating this to the customer, and an additional $300 was added to the bill without his approval.

When the customer came to pick up his car, he was furious, and rightly so. He said, "That is my rent money! How could you do this to me?" Of course, we removed the charge. It was an honest oversight, but a lack of clear communication no doubt damaged the trust we had established with this customer and led to a very bad experience.

Keeping Commitments

The number-one complaint in our business is not price. Rather, complaints come when we do not meet the commitment we made regarding the timing of when the job will be completed. When we keep our commitments on timing or communicate clearly well in advance of missing a deadline, we can keep relationships intact and help our customers feel valued. Keeping commitments proved very important for a customer who needed her car back in time to pick up her young daughter from school. When she dropped off her Camry, she was told the car would be ready in time; however, while replacing some suspension parts, a very rusty piece unexpectedly broke. Knowing we had committed to an important deadline, we scrambled to find a replacement part quickly. Rather than waiting for the part to be delivered a few hours later, we sent a driver 45 minutes away to get the part so we could meet the deadline and keep our commitment. Of course, this mom was thrilled.

Being Willing and Able to Ask for the Sale

Once our salespeople know what the customer needs, they are trained to be kind and direct when asking for the sale. If the customer needs it, they need it. There is no reason to dance around it. We typically say, "We can get started on it today. Can I get it done for you?" If the customer has budget concerns, we offer financing. If they can't wait to have their car serviced, we offer to get them a ride back to work. Most people appreciate a clear and direct invitation, so they know what we are able to accomplish. When you have established yourself as a strong sales organization, you will train your people not to be afraid to ask for the sale.

The Type of People a Sales-Driven Organization Employs

So, how do you attract sales-driven, enthusiastic, proactive team players who know how to apply the sales principles I have just outlined? I recommend looking for associates with the following characteristics:

People Who Are Willing to Learn

One thing that annoys me so much is when an associate says, "I've been doing this a long time, and . . ." When I hear this phrase, my brain immediately shuts off. Maybe it's because I have often been younger than many of my co-workers, but I have very little patience for that phrase, which is simply code for, "I'm too lazy to change," or, "I'm too stubborn to learn something new."

A good sales-driven organization looks for people who are hungry to learn more about sales. When it comes to the sales process, another phrase that is banned in our organization is, "That's the way we've always done it." People I work with never use this phrase, at least not anymore. I question every process all the time. I ask, "Why?" constantly. Everything we do is subject to change. I like what railroad executive Alfred Edward Perlman said about this: "After you've done a thing the same way for two years, look it over carefully. After five years, look at it with suspicion. And after ten years, throw it away and start all over." A good sales organization is chock full of people who are willing to change, evolve, adapt, and learn. In our company, we presume that no one has arrived, and no one knows it all; people who get stuck in their ways tend to find their way out of our company.

One way I have learned to test whether managers, leadership, and sales associates are willing to learn new things, so they can treat the business like a sales organization, is to send a top associate to a location and see what happens to numbers while they are there. In chapter 1, I highlighted one such location, which had struggled in the past to find a manager who treated the business like a sales company, so I sent Reese Carter to that shop for a week to see what would happen with him there.

As you may recall, without Reese there that store averaged $5,800 per day in sales. On Reese's first day, that location brought in $12,810, and after one week, it was averaging over $12,000 per day. Nothing else at the store changed whatsoever, other than a top sales-driven manager working there with them. The store had the same mechanics, the same tire technicians, the same products and services, and the same customer base. It was the sales mindset that Reese brought with him and trained others to have that made the difference.

This experience made it clear to me that some people are able to drive sales and others are not. This is largely due, in my opinion, to how *willing* and open managers and associates are to learn and apply proven principles. While these skills can be taught and you can try to train others to learn them, people still have to be open and *willing* to apply the concepts.

People Who Are Positive

We live with mistakes and we retrain. The employees who get weeded out most quickly on our sales teams are not those who are trying despite their errors; it's those who are negative. We have worked hard to recruit optimistic, brightly lit salespeople; our culture is largely one of positive energy, so we expect this same energy to be apparent across all the departments of our organization.

Our shop crews are driven and want to be busy, and if the sales associates feed them sales, they will get the work done, so we have to ensure that our salespeople have the right attitude that will allow this work to flow freely into our shops. If our salespeople don't have a positive outlook, it affects everything. That's why, when I want to reform a business, I always start with the sales associates first. We train, train, train, and if they have zero interest in trying our systems, understanding that we are a sales company first, and approaching their work with positivity so that everyone can stay busy and productive, they usually find somewhere else to work.

In each of the preceding chapters, I have highlighted some of the wonderfully positive and energetic people I have the opportunity to work with. If you don't have these kinds of people surrounding you, people like Reese and Robbie Carter and Jose and Miriam Cordova, I urge you to take a closer look at your sales force and make changes where needed.

People with Integrity

Just like me, I'm sure you are in this for the long haul and are building something that means more than just potential profits. In a true sales-driven company, making a buck should not be the top priority and should not be the purpose that drives your organization: It's people that matter, both those who work for you and those you do work for, no matter their circumstance. If you are trying to build a successful sales organization, there should be no tolerance for associates who intentionally deceive customers or try to take advantage of them. In our company we look for people who have integrity and who share our same ideals.

One evening, a customer came into the store with a flat tire and a damaged wheel. He was hoping to find some used replacements, but we didn't have the tires and it was near closing time so there was no way to find anything that night. He was very distraught because he had very little money. He was a very interesting, humble man who told us he had grown up in the inner city on the East Coast. The sales associate, Mike, saw that his car was full of blankets and garbage, and that's when we realized the man was living in his vehicle. The man told Mike that he was staying at the homeless shelter that night and had a ride to work in the morning; if we could put a tire and wheel on his car the next day, he would pick it up in the afternoon. Mike told him it would be about $80 for a used tire and a new wheel, and he said that would be fine.

The next day, Mike was able to find a used wheel and tire that cost just $20, and when the man came to pick it up later that day, he told him about the reduced charge. The customer stood there for a moment, and then tears began to stream down his cheeks. Mike asked him if he was okay and he said, "I'm just so grateful that you took the time to save me that money. Now I can buy some food. Thank you."

Store manager Elliott Simon, Miriam Cordova, and our technicians at our Bountiful, Utah, location demonstrated integrity when a customer came in asking for a particular repair. The repair would cost about $1,100. After some diagnostic work, our team discovered that some wiring was damaged; fixing that wiring reduced the service time by a couple of days. Elliott called the customer to tell him that his vehicle was ready and it would cost much less than anticipated. Here is the transcript of the voicemail I received from the customer:

"Miriam and Elliott are an amazing team, and your group down there is awesome. They could've taken me for a ride of over $1,000 on my truck, and it ended up costing me $140. I was blown away at the service I got. They're a really impressive team with a lot of personality and a genuine kindness. Thanks for everything."

Elliott

This might seem like just basic, honest customer service, but it doesn't always work like this in our industry. It takes people with integrity to make sure the right decisions are made when the business owner isn't there.

Working with people who care about customers is very important in a sales-driven organization. Of course, we made no money off the small tire replacement for the homeless man or the $140 truck repair, but that didn't matter. What mattered was Mike's behavior toward this customer, and Elliott and Miriam's attitude toward the truck owner. How you treat the people who choose to do business with you, no matter if you make a large sale or a very small one, ultimately affects the bottom line, and more importantly the opportunity for future success of all those involved in your organization.

People Who Are Hungry for More

Five years ago, Kory and I purchased an existing Goodyear Tire store. This store had a loyal clientele and consistent revenue; however, by my standards, their $900,000 in annual revenue needed to be improved. Working with the existing crew, I tried to teach them how to increase sales, work more efficiently, and fix more cars.

On the first day we owned the store, a Monday, I sat quietly to the side, listening to the sales associates. At that moment, there were four guys working in the shop and two cars in the bays. A potential customer called and asked when she could come in for an oil change. The associate pulled out a large notebook, flipped some pages, and said he could work her in on Thursday afternoon. Looking out at the empty shop and empty parking lot, I was shocked. When I asked him about the scheduling strategy, he explained that the guys in the shop didn't like it when things got too busy and complained if too many cars stacked up.

That evening, I had a meeting with the team. I tried to pump them up in a positive way and told them we were going to double sales immediately, which would mean everyone would make more money as that happened. Of the six total employees, two were excited. Four looked at the ground and cursed under their breath. Our transitional manager, Reese Carter, hired more people who wanted to grow the business, and as we worked together on sales techniques and work-flow, sales immediately shot up. We did not even have a new sign on the building, yet even with a nameless location, sales doubled imme-diately because of people who were hungry to grow and do a better job fixing people's cars.

I gave the four original associates with bad attitudes every chance to adapt and change to the new, faster pace, but they hated it. Within a few months, all four of them were gone for one reason or another. They had no hunger or desire for improvement, and they naturally found other places to go that fit what they were looking for.

After Reese's amazing transition period, we hired a permanent manager, Tyler Nickel. With a new attitude and new positive energy, that store did $2.5 million in revenue in its first full year, $3 million its second year, $4 million a couple of years later, and it continues to grow. The principal difference between its $900,000 starting point and where it is today is the attitude of the people working to make that location great.

Tyler

The Psychology of Mental Hunger

I have noticed that individuals with this bright energy also seem to have a ravenous appetite for greatness, which makes it possible for such people to achieve more than the average person. Dr. Craig Manning, a mental strength coach, recalls an experience from his youth where he learned about mental hunger. He describes the psychology of this mental hunger in his book *The Fearless Mind*, where he tells about his time as a teenage tennis player who had the opportunity to train with some of the best players in Australia. One of them was Patrick Rafter, who later became number one in the world and won the U.S. Open twice.

Manning noticed right away that Rafter was different from the other guys. He wasn't a strong player compared to others in their training group, yet he seemed to have something about his mental energy that was not easy to describe. "[Even though] the most successful [person] on the team at one time was the weakest (Patrick was not the biggest physically), he had the greatest weapon anyone could have: his mind was fearless." Rafter had learned to be mentally hungry. He was, as it says in the 13th century Icelandic Laxdoela sagas, "A hungry wolf . . . bound to wage a hard battle."

Removing Mental Limiters

People like Patrick Rafter, who are hungry like a wolf, are vital to organizations that strive to be sales-driven companies. But that hunger is not enough. Along with hiring people who are positive, energetic, and have this ravenous appetite for success, you also need to surround yourself with people who know how to remove mental limiters.

Mental limiters are much like the speed limiter, called the "governor" installed in most vehicles at the factory. Fuel-injected cars usually have these governors, which force them to top out at speeds of 100 to 150 miles per hour as a safety measure. Governors work through electronic sensors and the engine computer to slow down the vehicle as it reaches high speeds.

The human mind also has governors. Similar to cars, the brain's limiter is a safety measure to help us avoid excessive risk that could put us in physical or mental danger. The strength of this limiter varies from person to person and impacts each individual's appetite for risk, but we all have this governor. While its purpose is to keep us from serious injury, death, and even mental trauma, in some cases this limiter can keep us from performing at our highest capacity. Many times, people think they are maxed out at their highest and best, when in reality, they could do so much more.

The mental limiter works by using recent experience to estimate what future experiences will be like. If I crashed on my bike and flipped over the handlebars as a kid, for instance, my mental governor might make me think I will take a similar fall while riding my bike as an adult. Every time I put on the brakes, I brace myself for this possibility in order to protect myself. At work, if I sell $1,000 worth of tires today, for example, my brain thinks I will sell $1,000 of tires tomorrow. This is a safe place for my brain to remain, where it is comfortable and already knows certain details. Without this mental limiter, we can become very anxious about the uncertainty of life, so we stay where we think we already know what the outcome will be.

In his book *Endure: Mind, Body, and the Curiously Elastic Limits of Human Performance,* Alex Hutchinson, human endurance specialist, explains how the brain is constantly telling the body to perform at a safe level, a level that has been previously achieved. He says, "What's crucial is the need to override what your instincts are telling you to do (slow down, back off, give up). . . . Endurance implies something more sustained: holding your finger in the flame long enough to feel the heat." The brain is very conservative; it does not recognize what it can do until it has done it. People who can outsmart their own mental limiter are able to reach heights they've never even considered before.

In a sales-driven organization, mental limiters have to be removed as well. In our company, we have determined that we control our sales: It is up to us to choose to make sales increase, even if they weren't high the day before, week before, or even months or years before! When sales are down for a couple of weeks, I will sometimes hear people say, "Well, it's the economy," or, "it's the weather." They name some other outside force over which they have no control. Of course, outside forces can have an impact here and there, but the general trajectory, either downward or upward, is a choice.

When sales are down, we have trained associates to first ask, "What could I have done differently?" During the COVID-19 spread in 2020, most areas of the country were hit somewhat hard economically, and some were completely decimated. Even in such difficult circumstances, where an outside force clearly had an impact on sales, we still chose not to let our numbers slide as much as our neighbors'. In times like these, I urge you to ask, "What can I control? What can I do better tomorrow than I did today?"

Even in the worst conditions, I still know that I have control of my mindset and execution, and I do all I can to take off any mental limiters so I can go as far as possible under the circumstances. My son

Carson is, I think, an ideal example of what can happen when you take off your mental limiter.

As he entered his junior year of high school, Carson was an average distance runner on a very good high school team. During his freshman and sophomore years, he seemed to have decent running athleticism but was not on the varsity team (the top seven runners). While practicing with the team, he could keep up with most of the top runners but was nowhere near those same guys at the cross country meets.

During the summer between his sophomore and junior year in high school, 16-year-old Carson wanted to run a half-marathon (13.1 miles) just for fun, to see what he could do. I drove him an hour away at 4 a.m. to a race with a thousand adult participants. The event started while I took a nap in my truck. Having set my alarm, I woke up an hour later and sauntered toward the finish line with no idea how long it would take Carson to come in. The leader just approaching was a 27-year-old who sprinted past me and finished the race. Suddenly, I saw Carson coming around the corner, barreling down the street in second place! He looked relaxed and strong, but I did not expect him so quickly so I didn't have a camera ready to prove it. He finished the race at a 5:55-mile pace, around the same speed he had run previous 5K (3.1 mile) races. No other teenagers were in the top ten. I asked him how he felt, and he said, "Amazing! I didn't feel any pressure, I just ran!"

Obviously, Carson's mental limiter was off during this half-marathon, and he completed the race with a phenomenal time. On a cool summer morning in the Wasatch Mountains, away from the scrutiny of his peers among people he didn't know, his mind was free to relax and achieve something he had not before considered possible.

A month later, during a fundraiser 5K for Carson's school team, I could see him getting tense as he ran. The pressure of a race against his teammates was on his mind, and the mental limiter was back in full force. He ran that race in 17:31 and finished twelfth on his team. His 5:40 pace was still respectable but unfortunately light-years from other elite runners' times.

A few weeks later, Carson was set to run in the first real meet of the season, an invitational with about 20 high schools on a beautiful golf course at the mouth of Ogden Canyon in Ogden, Utah. Before the race, Carson looked like death: He was pale, nervous, and tight. I asked him to think about how he felt before his half-marathon and what was going through his mind at that time. He said, "I just had fun." I then said to him, "Let's get one thing straight: This is not the Olympics, this is not life or death, this is high school. All of these races are just for fun."

At the shot of the starter's gun, Carson took off in the junior varsity 5K with hundreds of other kids. I did not know he had set a goal to win the race, but it soon became obvious that his mental limiter came off; he ran with more fun than fear and finished with an amazing time of 15:48, ending up with a first-place gold medal in the junior varsity division. His time was the seventh-fastest on his entire team, including the runners in the varsity race. I asked him how he did it, and he said, "I just told myself it would be fun to go faster, and if I had to drop out halfway through, I would." Turning his mental limiter down had proved to him that it was possible to go further than he had ever supposed before.

A month later, in Boise, his team participated in the Bob Firman Invitational, a huge meet with nearly 100 high schools from all over the western United States. In this race, he ran a new personal record at a 5:10-mile pace and had the third-best time on his team.

At Utah's Region 1 meet a few weeks later, he set a goal to remove the mental limiter even more and to keep up with the fastest senior on his team for as long as he could. He did not know if he would be able to do it, but he was going to try. With this mental hunger and positive attitude, he was able to finish fourth in the region, which qualified him for the Utah State Championship Meet. He was now second place on his team, two seconds behind the leader. Seconds after crossing the finish line he said, "I think I could have gone faster!"

In October of that year at the high school state championship, he wanted to be the fastest runner on his team. He did, in fact, pass the top runner in the final 100 meters to reach that goal. He also finished twelfth in the state in the 6A division. In 60 days, Carson had gone from being twelfth on his team to twelfth in the state. By the following spring, he ran the 1600m in 4:21, took fourth in the state, and was the top junior in the state for 6A. Now graduated from high school, Carson enjoys running at a Division 1 university.

We all have mental limiters—little voices in our head that tell us what we can and cannot do. We have distracting thoughts that say we aren't able to do more than what we have already done. The messages these voices nitpick us with aren't valid. While they are naturally there to protect us from harming ourselves, they also lie about our actual abilities. They are based on what we have done in the past, not on what we can accomplish in the future. Like Carson, we can all break through these artificial, self-imposed limits. We can tell our brain that it is wrong and always do much more than we think we can.

A Sales-Driven Organization Always Strives to Stay Relevant

In addition to surrounding yourself with willing, positive, mentally hungry people to create a successful sales-driven organization, you also need to stay relevant. What this means is that everything you do must match what you are trying to accomplish. When people used to ask me what business I was in, I said I was in the business of fixing vehicles. But I have learned since that this isn't really relevant and that we are actually in the business of *selling* repairs on vehicles. We are first and foremost a sales organization, and everything we do must work harmoniously with this identity. After all, if we have no sales, we have no business.

Our primary way of staying relevant in all our Big O Tires stores is through our people. Building a sales team with a positive, can-do mindset that allows us to push our sales goals forward is fun. You may think that finding these kinds of people—people who want to push themselves—is too hard, and perhaps you have been discouraged at times. I hear from business owners that this new generation of workers just doesn't care, that they don't have drive, that they don't have work ethic like *we* used to. Some of this may be true, but if you've assumed this attitude about potential hires, I'd like to propose that perhaps you are imposing a mental limiter on yourself and the people you employ. Perhaps it's time to look at things from a different angle. The angle I try to see things from, and what I believe, is that most people want to be great. If I can help them see the vision of what they are capable of doing, help them see that they are much more than they think, and then reward them accordingly, many will rise to the occasion. And in the process, they will help us stay relevant as a sales-driven organization and help push our company beyond perceived limits to greater heights.

Building a team with key people who understand we are a sales organization first allowed 2018 to be monumental for our company. For the first time since 2006, the 9th South store was the number-one location in the national Big O Tires chain, with sales of $7,513,432—almost four times that of the national average, which is $2,000,000.

After setting that new record in 2018, I told my team at that store the story of Carson's distance running and that we needed to remove our mental limiters because we would soon be hitting $10 million . . . and that would be just the beginning.

It is my belief that when you approach the work you do with this type of mental hunger and hire people who share your same drive, your company can become a sales-driven organization where the sky's the limit and records are broken every year. As Peruvian author and entrepreneur Rodolfo Costa has said, "Cultivate an optimistic mind, use your imagination, always consider alternatives, and dare to believe that you can make possible what others think is impossible."

In chapter 5, I want to share some details about how to value your customers, which goes hand-in-hand with building a successful sales organization. While these strategies and techniques may seem small, they can have a pretty big impact on the success of your business.

5

Little Things Are Big Things, Especially When It Comes to Valuing the Customer

"The way you do small things is the way to do all things."

—Jens Wolff

I think I've made it clear by now that I am not a car person . . . I am not a mechanic. I am not a tire-lover. I do not know the size of the engine in my truck. When my neighbors ask me about a car issue (my family knows better), I stare blankly before telling them I have no clue how to answer their question. I truly enjoy the business I am in, but I'm a bit of an outsider compared to the many incredible experts in my industry.

However, this lack of knowledge—and lack of upbringing in the automotive world—has given me a unique perspective and has been a huge advantage for me. Why? Because I know what it's like to be the customer. I have been the customer. My ideas and strategies for how to work with and serve our customers have been formed, in part, from my experience being one myself. My first time walking into a tire store with a very limited budget to buy tires for my white 1996 Geo Prizm is still the lens through which I view much of the way I want my team to interact with our customers.

In addition to understanding how a customer thinks and feels, I've also been influenced in my approach to our clientele by what I've learned about the importance of truly *valuing* the people who walk through my shop doors. As I have tried to share in this book, valuing people, on a much deeper level than what commonly occurs in most business operations, is what determines whether an organization will grow or not, will prosper or not, will become the best it can possibly be . . . or not.

As I first shared in the introduction, it was Jose Cordova who taught me that valuing people is more important than anything else you do to succeed in your business. The idea that "It's not about the mangos" became a guiding light to show me just how important people—especially customers—are if you want to create a healthy company culture and organizational success.

Through the Mango Principle, Jose showed me that it wasn't the size of the fruit he was selling, the price he charged, or how hard he hustled someone that made him the number-one mango salesperson in his town in Mexico. It was about how he treated the customers who lined up to buy fruit from him—and only him. It was about the relationship he built with those people: how he asked about their family and work, how he used humor to put them at ease, how he related to them. This made all the difference. "*It's not about what you're selling,*" Jose taught me, "*it's all about connections—it's all about people.*"

In the end, no matter how successful you are at building a team of positive, hard-working people dedicated to making the sale, if you don't know or respect what the customer feels or value what they mean to your organization, none of that really matters. CEO of the customer strategy consulting firm CXJourney, Annette Franz, said it best: "Putting the 'customer' in the *customer experience* means that you're thinking about the humans in front of you, listening to them, understanding them, designing the experience for them. And it's a reminder that without customers, you have no business."

Valuing customers is the last piece, so to speak, of the "people matter puzzle" that goes along with all the other ideas I have explained in the previous chapters. This puzzle piece must also be in place if you want to create a strong company culture that can take your organization to the next level.

> **Organizational success is always based on how much you are willing to value other people, to lift them up, and to connect with them. This is especially true when it comes to the customers you serve, and it's often the little things that make all the difference in cultivating that relationship.**

Why the Little Things Are So Big

When you are bogged down with hiring and training issues, accounting matters, sales and marketing, and the other day-to-day concerns of running a business, putting processes in place that ensure you are providing the right customer experience may seem like a big chore. But surprisingly, being able to fit this piece into place doesn't require Herculean efforts. I have found that it's not the big things we do for our customers that are the most significant. Small actions add up and can ultimately result in massively successful outcomes. Humor, a kind word, a smile, a compliment, and genuine interest goes a long way. Most importantly, seeing your customer as more than just a way to make a sale is ironically one of the keys to getting that sale. We try to appreciate that people want to be seen and heard and not taken for granted. They want to know that they matter to you beyond the money in their pocket. They want to be treated as you would want to be treated. They want courtesy. They want respect.

When customers respond to the little things you do to make them sincerely feel this way, big things begin to happen. Trust is developed, which leads to a whole slew of amazing outcomes for your organization, beyond just increased sales. "When companies build trust, they enable customers . . . to advocate their business," says Mariah Raner in her March 2021 article for Brandcraft.com. Her point is that when customers can trust you, not only do they buy from you, but they also take some of the marketing and sales work off your shoulders by evangelizing your company and getting others to come buy from you as well. "These customer evangelists [help] increase brand visibility and attract more customers. Building trust establishes a stronger customer base, gives you a competitive edge, and cultivates continued growth."

Turns out, organizational trust is important, and the way that trust is cultivated depends on how well you handle the little things. These little things will determine whether big things like customer loyalty are developed and whether a solid relationship can be grown and maintained with you over time.

Little Things That Are Big

In previous chapters, we explored together several basic practices you can implement that can affect the type of people you attract and work with to build your organization into a successful business. Many of the simple ways you help your associates and team members feel needed and valued within the organization can also be applied to the way you treat your customers and the type of positive experience you create for them.

Love People

Okay, I said it before: The "l-word" in a business setting may seem corny, but if loving your team is effective on the inside, it can also be very beneficial when you interact in this way with your customers, who are coming to you from the outside.

"Can my company really 'love' its customers?" you may be asking. Well, yes. I think it can, so long as you are genuine in the way you express it. There are many people who have undying love for their favorite companies and products, so I'm assuming that same feeling of love and loyalty can be reciprocated for your customers and vendors. After all, the customer is the lifeblood of your business and must be valued as such.

In our company, we shoot for top-notch efficiency, effective marketing and sales, and a positive, energetic business culture in which our associates can thrive. But treating the customer the way we would like to be treated has the biggest impact on the organization's growth and development.

Here are some of the ways we have tried to "show the love" to our customers:

- **Use courteous language.** You would think that this goes without saying, but there seems to be many businesses out there that don't know or care to train their employees about being civil with customers. The old basics of "please" and "thank you" go a long way. I am surprised these days by the number of store clerks, for example, who don't even look at you after the transaction is completed, let alone say "thank you" when they hand you your receipt.

  Using courteous language also means never losing your temper. Unless someone comes into your establishment threatening people with violence, there's never really much reason to yell or get heavy-handed with a customer, even if they are angry, difficult, or hard to satisfy.

- **Recognize, always and every day, that customers could choose to take their business elsewhere** and that they may be going through challenges you cannot see (refer to the next section, "Treat Each Customer Like They Are the Only One You Will Ever Serve"), so be careful not to criticize behavior.

- **Don't judge customers based on their appearance.** Remember the homeless man I mentioned in the last chapter who desperately needed an affordable tire? Every customer is worthy of your best efforts.

- **The right connections matter.** Understand that each person who comes through your door is going to connect with you and your company in a different way, so be sure to hook them up with team members who can best help them feel at ease and make the customer experience enjoyable. This may mean reassigning sales or projects if the current arrangement isn't working.

Treat Each Customer Like They Are the Only One You Will Ever Serve

I bet, just like me, that you have known someone—at one point or another—who has made you feel like you were the most important person in their life (I love being around people like this!). You know they have family, friends, and business associates who are very significant to them, but there's just something about the way they engage with you, respond to your thoughts, and treat you with respect that makes you feel like you are the only person in the world that matters to them at that moment.

This feeling of focused, intentional value they place on you is the type of attention that any business of decent caliber should give every customer it deals with. Just like building a team with positive energy is important, I believe that bringing light and enthusiasm to the customer experience is also important. The best way to do this is to never take any person who walks through your doors for granted.

If your team has the attitude that customers are a dime a dozen and there will always be another one lined up to give you business, it's time to do a little re-training. I mean in today's economic climate, who has the luxury to look at customers like that? I don't know about you, but I am really put off by someone who seems put out by having to serve me as part of their job. I love this quote by author and business trainer Laurie McIntosh: "You are serving a customer, not a life sentence. Learn how to enjoy your work." Don't make your customers feel like a burden; approach people with a positive, energetic attitude.

But what if you find yourself involved with a customer who is really hard to satisfy and your employees don't want to deal with them so they brush the person off? What happens next? In this age of abundant online interaction, it's so very easy for unhappy customers to spread all kinds of negative information on social media and across the web about your company's customer service. You can't afford to treat any client with indifference or disregard. Just as I noted in chapter 2, that it isn't smart in today's economy to let employees go for little infractions and assume that there will be another person to step up and take their place, it isn't a good business practice to treat any customer like they are unimportant and that another, better, and easier person to deal with will be right along.

Regard every person you interact with as if they are the only one you will ever serve.

Be Willing to Hear What Your Customers Think of You

As I mentioned in chapter 2, I have tried to create an environment where my team isn't afraid to speak candidly with me about any issues going on in our organization. I also work to make this open-door policy a given in my interactions with customers and vendors. Don't be afraid to ask your customers for feedback. Then sit back and listen. "Actively listening to people does more than earn trust—it earns loyalty and even love for who you are and what you do," says Robin Blakely, CEO of the brand strategy firm Creative Center of America. "So, listen. Make sure you hear properly. Ask relevant questions."

Many times in the past, my team assumed I was a weirdo as I creepily stood in the corner to just watch and think. Early on, they worried that I was watching them to try to catch them doing something wrong. But now they understand that I am just learning. I am listening to conversations with customers and vendors, watching their reactions, noticing their body language, and silently determining if what we are doing to make our customers feel valued is working.

Here are a few additional things you can do to make sure your customers sense that their opinions are valued. These small investments can lead to big dividends as your clientele feels more heard and understood. As you work to implement their suggestions, you just might discover new ways to do things you hadn't thought of before, including building a better product or innovating more effective ways to deliver your service. But beyond that, and more importantly, you will no doubt increase customer loyalty and ultimately set yourself up for greater growth and progress.

- **Customer Surveys:** Asking for customer feedback can be a great way to help your clientele feel valued. But be sure to request it non-intrusively, say the experts at iEduNote.com: "Shoving a questionnaire down [customer or vendor] throats preemptively is a bit heavy-handed, but if you have a place customers can easily access to leave feedback and how their experience was, that will pay off. You'll receive direct feedback from your customers, and they'll end up getting a more satisfying experience if you implement some fixes for them."

- **Online Commentary:** No one in any business, no matter how good their product or service is or how amazing their people are, is ever going to receive nothing but five-star reviews. We all know it is impossible to please all people, all the time. However, don't let this stop you from setting up simple ways for your customers and vendors to comment, rate, and refer you on your social media, website, and other online platforms. Then be sure to respond to those comments, both positive and negative.

So much due diligence and product research is now done online by potential customers, and they rely heavily on what other people have said about their experience working with you, including how you respond to negative feedback. Customers understand as well as you do that every review will not be five stars, but I think they are likely to be very forgiving of a company who can address any negative comments that they receive.

"Show them you are acting on their feedback," says *Forbes'* Coach Council writer, Annette Franz. "Tell them, 'We hear you and we're doing something about it.' When you ask customers for feedback, let them know that it was received, that you heard what they are saying and that you're going to do something with it."

Be Grateful and Express It

As I mentioned in chapter 2, gratitude is a little thing that although difficult for me to express verbally, is something actually quite simple to show and can go a long way toward helping people feel valued. Showing appreciation builds trust in your organization with the people who choose to do business with you and are loyal to your company.

Just like a paycheck alone isn't enough to demonstrate to your employees that you appreciate everything they do to help you build your business (see chapter 2), you can't assume that your outstanding product or service is enough to fully build loyalty and garner trust from your customers—they need to know that *you* truly appreciate their business as well. Sending handwritten thank-you notes to loyal customers and vendors, featuring clients on your social media sites and in your newsletter, and creating a referral program to reward frequent buyers can be great ways to show people your gratitude.

Value Customers by the Way You Sell to Them

The way you interact with customers during the sales process is one of the most important means by which you show them that you care and that they are important to you. The first three of the four sales principles I outlined in chapter 4 are directly tied to how you treat the customer (relationships of trust; clear communication; and keeping commitments), and even the fourth—asking for the sale—relates to how well you have executed the other three in terms of gaining the customer's trust and confidence that you have their best interest in mind and are not just schmoozing them to make a buck.

Let's review these sales principles in the context of valuing the customer to see how you can use them as a guide for treating people right during the sale:

Building Personal Relationships of Trust with Customers

One of the best ways I know of to create a trusting relationship with people is to make them feel comfortable about asking questions—any question. Let them feel like what they are wondering is okay to ask. Don't act like you don't have time for their inquiries. Make sure that if there's an education process to your product, either in buying it or using it, that they feel like you care enough to explain things to them; that you want to share; and that you have time for them.

Another way to build relationships of trust with your customers is to make the buying process pleasant. An article on iEduNote.com explains, "The entire process, from perusing your products to finalizing payment should be as smooth and enjoyable as possible, with clear indications of how much you'll charge and how to proceed at each step. If you manage to make buying things from you fun and easy, you've struck gold."

After the sale is finalized, checking in with a customer to see how things are going is also a great way to maintain the relationship. Stick to your clients in a non-aggressive way but in a way that says you're committed to them. When people hear from your organization *after* the sale, when there's really no incentive to reach out to them other than to show you care and want to be sure they are happy and satisfied, they know you truly value them as a person and appreciate their business.

Accurate and Clear Communication

One of the most important things you can do to show your customers that you value them is to be completely honest. "Always tell them the truth," urges Mark Savinson, a *Forbes* writer and consultant with a sales productivity consultancy firm. "Clients may not like the truth, they may not have the budget or resources to tackle the whole truth, but telling the truth enables you to work with them to make the best decisions and find the best outcomes based on their resources and priorities."

I think open, honest communication is especially important in my industry. Customers may sometimes get a little nervous when they turn over their car to have repair work done. Many people are very protective of their vehicle and worry if it will come back better than it did when they drove it into the shop or if there will be something new to worry about when they pick it up. They wonder if they can trust the mechanics performing various functions on their car and if the sales associate can be trusted to give them a fair deal. People need to have confidence that you will treat them fairly, and if you ask questions to understand their true concerns and needs, then explain your processes and products clearly, they are more likely to feel that you truly do care and want to do what's best for them.

In our organization, we practice how to ask questions and then listen to customer responses. Our general manager, Miriam Cordova, will pull an associate aside and interview her or him to test them on their ability to listen and to ask the right questions. It makes our people uncomfortable at first if they think we are trying to catch them at not knowing what they are doing. But they get more relaxed and embrace it more when they see that we are just working with them to help them better communicate with customers. We are a sales organization, and we train our people constantly on these techniques.

Keep Commitments

It is critical that you do what you say you'll do, *when* you say you'll do it. When people need their car, they need their car. But in actuality, it doesn't matter what type of business you operate: You should always follow through with what you promise the customer when you close the deal with them. This means you don't change the price or offer one set of services and give another. It means you don't promise the car, wedding dress, birthday cake, legal contract, new roof, food order, purchasing agreement, software app, coaching service, or anything else and then go back on that promise. Customers tend not to look too highly on companies that don't think their time or money is as important as the organization's.

A story one of my colleagues told me about her five-year-old daughter illustrates how important it is to keep commitments. Her child had broken her arm and was scheduled to have surgery at 1:30 in the afternoon to put pins in the elbow and repair the bone. Her little girl had to come to the hospital fasting, having not eaten anything since 9 p.m. the night before. She was already hungry, to be sure, when she arrived at the hospital, but as her 1:30 surgery time came and went, the hunger pangs got worse. Nurses were attentive and tried to keep the little girl occupied. My colleague lay in the pre-op bed with her daughter and read her stories and soothed her whenever she asked when she was going to get her arm fixed so she could eat.

Pretty soon it was three, then four, and the hospital explained that some emergency surgeries had to be done before hers. This was understandable to all the adults, but it wasn't fair to a child who had been fasting, by then, for 18 hours. Still, the little girl was very patient, never really complaining or whining about the delay.

By 6 p.m., it seems, my colleague's daughter was done. She sat up in bed and said without a tear, in a very corporate executive voice, "When is the surgery going to be done? I've had about enough of this." Then she began to bawl, and bawl hard. It was loud, and it was insistent, and my colleague told her daughter she had every right to cry as hard and as long as she wanted and let her do it, making sure the door was wide open. She could be heard all the way down the long hospital corridor, and sure enough, within 15 minutes her daughter was wheeled into surgery.

When you promise something, be sure to keep your commitments. The customer, in the end, will make sure you do, even if they have to make a stink about it. And in the end, promising to deliver what (and when) you say you will is just good business (and hospital) practice.

A Few More "Little Things" to Consider

Fix Mistakes Immediately and Move On

We all make mistakes. That's a given, but I bet what's not as easy is accepting that even when you don't make a mistake sometimes your customers think you have. We've certainly had our fair share of these moments. What I have learned is it doesn't matter who's at fault, and the best way to handle mistakes—no matter who or what's to blame—is to fix them in a reasonable way and move on.

In the past, I have observed some of my managers drag issues out for days in order to save a few hundred dollars, and it just causes brain damage. It is usually not worth drawing problems out to try and squeeze every dollar you can from the customer.

When we make a mistake, the goal is to get it fixed as fast as possible in order to move forward quickly. This means dealing with errors in a timely manner, but it also means coming up with quality solutions that leave the customers better off than when they first came to see us.

I view troublesome issues, like a vehicle that wears out tires a lot faster than normal, or a customer who says we damaged their car while it was in our care, as dark clouds hanging over the team, and I want them gone. They suck energy out of our organization and divert our attention from the positive activities we are trying to pursue to make our business more relevant. If I have taken the time to create a strong company culture and working environment in my stores where everything is built around optimism, efficiency, and positive energy, then I want to keep the focus on those things and quickly resolve the matters that drain us and can possibly damage our relationship with customers.

If everything hinges on making good connections and having positive interactions with the people who trust us with their time and money, then I see no need to hang onto any conflicts or complications any longer than necessary. When company heads and business owners do so, they end up sucking the life out of their organization in order to maintain what they assume is "control."

An incident that happened at one of our stores demonstrates why it is so important to resolve problems quickly and efficiently then move on. Some time back, one of our associates moved two vehicles that had been in the shop overnight out of the bays and into parking spaces at the far end of the parking lot. In the rush to get the store open, he left the keys in the vehicles with the intent of moving them back into the shop momentarily. Just then, two transient people happened to walk past the cars, hopped in them, and took off. The police found one car a few days later, 300 miles away, but with minimal damage—thankfully. The other vehicle was located ten days later in rough shape. The temporary user of the car had been living in it, doing drugs in it, and driving it into objects—it was totaled.

My team handled this incident like champs. They arranged rental cars, called insurance companies, and spoke with the customers to explain what we were doing to solve the problem. Obviously, the car owners were not thrilled, but they could see and feel our desire to rectify the problem quickly and effectively. While the incident was a serious misfortune that caused some distraction, the team took immediate action so they could move on to more positive opportunities quickly.

Some of the most challenging situations we must deal with are when a customer places strong blame squarely on our shoulders for something that falls into a gray area, where it is difficult to know who is at fault. For example, we had an older vehicle come in that had a lot of rusty suspension parts. The customer had a limited budget but really needed shocks and struts, which she agreed to purchase at a fair price. While our technician was replacing a strut, a rusty sway bar link (a small suspension part) snapped in half. While we could have told her up front that it is very common for rusty sway bar links to break during this type of repair, we did not tell her that. So, we had to consider this question: Did the part break because it was old and rusty and the break was inevitable (normal wear and tear), or was it because the technician didn't take enough care when he replaced the strut (our fault)? The customer strongly insisted, "You broke it so you should pay for it!" In this case, we replaced the part for free and moved on. I have always found that quibbling over these "gray areas" of blame is a huge time-waster and can be very risky in terms of maintaining your relationship with the customer. What works best for our organization is to give the client the benefit of the doubt, to err on the side of caution, and to be sure we help them feel heard and understood. It's not worth it to me to go to war over forty dollars or a few hundred dollars. If I can meet them in the middle, I will suggest that; if not, I take care of the problem quickly.

It's Not Just about the Money (or the Mangos)

I mentioned in chapter 2 that the motivation to treat your associates and management team members well should not just be about bringing in profits hand over fist, and the same applies to your customers: If you are acting in an inauthentic way toward your clients, they will see right through you. Customers who feel genuinely valued will remain loyal to you, which of course does affect your bottom line but also brings benefits having to do with much more than just money.

"Business transactions can easily become impersonal, so extending even the smallest amount of courtesy by treating your customer like a distinct human being instead of a dollar sign pays dividends," says an iEduNote.com expert. "Any small detail counts, so long as it demonstrates you astutely paid attention to every detail about them that you could . . . make it personal."

This kind of genuine care creates connections and, as I mentioned earlier in the chapter, builds trust in your organization. It ensures other kinds of business success that are vital to keeping your organization going strong over the long haul.

Decluttering Your Business: One of the Best Ways to Show You Care

This may seem like a strange piece of advice, but the way you present yourself has a lot to do with showing the customer how much you value them.

In assisting and observing thousands of customers over the years, I have come to the following conclusion about clutter in a shop or on a website: Rarely does a customer look at a poster or display and ask about the particular product or service being advertised. Many times, they already know what they want when they enter your establishment, and if they don't know what they want then they are looking for a human being to help them figure it out. They don't walk into an automotive repair shop, for example, and examine a brake system display then say, "So, I was inspecting the brake display over there and I was wondering if you could look at my brakes for me?" Yes, it has happened . . . but almost never.

I've also observed that in my industry product brands are not super relevant to most customers (although this does depend on the type of business you are in). For instance, very few people getting their vehicle serviced care that I have a particular battery brand on my wall or a certain strut brand staring at them. Customers do not see those things because they aren't relevant to them.

What customers do see when they walk in your doors or get onto your website, however, is clutter. They see things they don't care about. Some people will disagree with me on this matter and argue that their customers love knowing that they carry a particular brand of brakes or tires or struts, or whatever it is they are selling. When it comes to most after-market car parts, the vast majority do not care that much about brand. For one week, the service writers at our various locations took notes on what questions each customer asked when they shopped for tires and other replacement parts. Out of 267 people who shopped for tires, only 39 were brand-conscious (where brand played a significant role in their decision). That's about 15%. Even more telling, only about 2% of customers asked for a specific brand on other replacement parts. While a small number of customers get really excited about certain brands of tires, most customers ask the same three questions about tires, in this order:

How many miles do they get?

What is the price?

How long will it take to put them on?

Then, maybe they'll ask about the brand of the tires. What generally happens is that in a ten-year period, one or two people are interested in a display, so a business owner thinks it's effective. Or a small number of brand-enthusiasts, who are really into a particular brand of brake pads, cause a store manager to think most customers are really particular about brake pad brands. What I believe is that the vast majority of people prefer cleanliness and less clutter when they enter your site, whether it's your brick-and-mortar shop or your online web store.

What they need to notice instead of clutter is whether there's anyone around to answer their questions, how responsive and courteous those people are, and whether the store clerk, customer service rep, or sales associate is going to make a genuine connection with them or not. Successful business, after all, isn't about the mangos (or the display, wall art, office or shop design, website interactive graphics, or even that much about your product or service)—it's about the connection you are making with your customers and whether they understand how much you really care . . . or don't. When we create a great experience for the customer they will remember the important brand that we care most about, which is our brand, the brand on our store.

In the age of information overload, people need less to think about, analyze, and process when they come into your establishment. Make it easier for them to do business with you by getting rid of extraneous clutter, both physical and mental. I always like to tell all my shop managers, "Remember, less is more" and "just keep it simple" when it comes to what customers must visually process during their experience in our stores.

Of course, my perspective comes from the automotive industry, but I think it can also apply across a wide variety of businesses. I think having to evaluate too many things can distract and fatigue the mind. Unless you are operating a business where customers won't feel comfortable without a ton of choices (such as a grocery store, where empty shelves tend to make people very nervous), I recommend simplifying your showroom and online spaces.

I have been in other stores (all kinds, not necessarily tire stores) in which shop keepers think they are not cluttered, but I beg to differ. To me, things lying around on the countertops and tacked up on walls, along with too many purchasing options, distracts and fatigues the mind, as I said earlier.

I was recently consulting for a small-engine power equipment store, where they sell lawnmowers, snowblowers, trimmers, and chainsaws. They were paying a lot of rent for a large showroom and featuring an enormous number of equipment models. The store manager assumed they needed to have every possible brand and model on display.

When I first walked in the store as a non-expert, I felt immediately overwhelmed by all the choices and wanted to leave, thinking that if I were a customer coming in to buy my next lawnmower it would be too much work to figure out what to purchase. I told the owner that customers like a few choices (good, better, best), but not too many, and recommended that he choose three to four of the top sellers for each brand and get rid of the rest. I was pretty confident this would increase sales for him and on top of that decrease his overhead.

He took my advice and cleaned everything up. Keeping it clean and simple has helped their business tremendously. They were able to decrease their leased space by 30 percent, saving significant rent, and sales have gone up.

When we declutter at our Big O Tires stores, we really declutter. Vendors are constantly sending us elaborate displays and flashy posters, and I throw them all away. I view them all as useless clutter. I do not believe that people read them or care about them. They are boring, and our minds are now trained to tune out advertising, especially boring ads. Instead, I try to use appealing images that are fun, calming, or soothing. Our stores are styled more like a coffee shop than a car shop. Think Apple stores. Think Starbucks. Think clean and concise. What about your establishment and online sites? Are they styled in such a way as to be appealing to your wide customer base?

When I take over an existing location, the first thing I do is fill the dumpster (or two or three) full of worthless, distracting junk from the showroom. Everything comes off the counters, everything comes off the walls. Perhaps now is a good time to ask yourself what you might need to get rid of in your own place of business. What do you need to do to make the shopping and service experience for your customers easy, no-nonsense, and enjoyable? If you're not sure, I urge you to think about your store and website. How cluttered are they, really? As Albert Einstein once said, "Out of clutter, find simplicity. From discord, find harmony."

Incoming Phone Calls

While many customers shop online these days, several people will still use the phone to get information about you and your business. Sometimes people just want to hear an actual human voice and to see how quickly they can get the service or product they need. Online shopping and information gathering is great to a point, but let's face it: it is very impersonal. Depending on the type of business you are operating, it might not facilitate great customer relations or even make sales.

Sometimes people just want to know they aren't hanging out in cyberspace, without a single human who is even remotely aware of their needs or what they are looking to buy or accomplish. Often, it can feel like there is no way of really connecting with anyone about the purchasing or evaluating process.

Humans crave connection with other humans so until the specialized artificial intelligence (AI) being created and tested to automate some sales processes comes in to fully replace your people, show your customers some real human love by the way you interact with them on the phone. While AI is already being used to streamline telemarketing and sales in some companies and humanoid sales robots are getting closer to being integrated by some industries to replace your sales associates on the floor (see the newest research in books like *The Selling Revolution*), human interaction during the sales process, especially on the phone, continues to be very important.

How you handle calls with the customer, though seemingly small, can actually be huge. In our case, incoming phone calls are still the mainstay of our organization. We are obsessed with being great on the phone, and it has changed our business. Here's how we use the phone to efficiently serve our customers:

- Make appointments to visit with people face-to-face when possible and on a video call where it's not. People are busy. People want to schedule stuff. Set an appointment so they know they matter to you. If you're busy, figure out a way to get them taken care of in a timely manner. When someone says, "We don't take appointments; it is first-come, first-served," it makes people who are not the first feel unimportant and unappreciated. We avoid that phrase. An easy solution in our case, where the customer has to give up their car for a time, is to offer a ride-share service back to their work or home so they don't have to sit and wait.

- Ask them what they are looking for and then just listen. Many times, it can be tempting to jump right into a sales pitch before you really understand what the customer wants. For example, when someone calls our shop and says they're looking for tires, it can be tempting to launch into the benefits of a certain brand. Instead, we train our people to ask a follow-up question such as, "Is there something specific you are looking for?" or, "Can you tell me more about what you're hoping to find? I want to make sure I find a solution that's just right for you." Then we just listen.

- Leave them on a high note such as, "Thanks so much for giving me a call. I'd love to have your business."

Once you have given it your best shot on the phone, the only way to know if what you are doing is working is to record phone calls and listen to them to see what you might need to do to make the customer experience better and to help in training service and sales associates.

Step Away

All of these small things add up. By working to improve each of these little things, the results can be big. When you are really dialed into each of these strategies, it's almost guaranteed you'll improve your customer service processes, build more trust into your organization, and, of course, ultimately make more profit. However, I know it can be difficult to work on so many details. When I had one store, it was often very hard just to survive each day, let alone become great at so many little things having to do with valuing the people around me.

One thing that helped me was to let go of some of the day-to-day control of the business. I have learned that I must trust my team. I teach them how our stores should look, how we will treat people, and how we will sell our products and services; then I get out of the way. While the team executes the strategy, I can then step away to evaluate the big picture issues. Andrew Carnegie said, "No man will make a great business who wants to do it all himself, or to get all the credit of doing it. That spirit is fatal, and the sure proof of a small mind."

Stepping away can be one of the best things you can do to help your business become better. By stepping away, I can see more, and my mind has more time to notice patterns and think through solutions. It allows me the time and creative energy that I—as a business owner—need in order to regroup, revise, re-strategize and put new plans in place that can help my company work better and more efficiently on the little things. Remember, all of these little things will add up, eventually having a major positive impact on your organization.

In conclusion, I want to share something that religious leader Carl W. Buehner once said about the importance of valuing people: "I've learned that people will forget what you said, people will forget what you did, but people will never forget how you made them feel." When your customers can feel that they truly matter to you, they will line up to buy what you have to offer, just like they did with Jose. The way he treated his customers was not *what* he did; it was really a part of *who* he is. As the former vice president and general manager of Nordstrom, Betsy Sanders said, "Service, in short, is not what you do, but who you are. It's a way of living that you need to bring to everything you do if you're to bring it to your customer interactions."

The little things you do make a difference. Over time, they get woven into the fabric of the organization and take on a life of their own, becoming entire infrastructures that support the way you do business so you can keep it moving forward.

In the next and final chapter, I want to share with you how surrounding yourself with people who believe they can influence their outcomes can help create a dynamic company culture that has the power to take your organization to places you never dreamed possible.

6

The Power of People Who Believe They Can Influence Their Outcomes

"Good thoughts and actions can never produce bad results;
bad thoughts and actions can never produce good results.
This is but saying that nothing can come from corn but
corn, and nothing from nettles but nettles."

—James Allen

No matter how successful an organization is, every company can fall into a slump at times. There will always be opposition in all things, and onto every life and every organization a little rain must fall. This has been true for our business as well. While we have enjoyed a mostly upward climb since things started to turn around at the 9th South store in 2010, there have been times when I've felt like we've hit a wall. Sometimes it seems we've done all we can but still aren't progressing as much as we should, and the only thing I can do is hang on and not lose what ground we've already gained. It can be hard for any company to experience such periods of stagnation and uncertainty.

At times like these in our organization, when it's been tough to ignore the mental limiters and I've needed help pulling out of brief periods of discouragement, I've learned to turn to people who believe they can influence their outcomes. One such person, whose phenomenal attitude and accomplishments I have shared with you throughout this book, is my brother-in-law Jason Hall.

Jason has always been an inspiration to me, ever since he started dating my sister when I was 14 years old. After an amazing life—spent mostly in a wheelchair—having influenced people all over the world with his infectious optimism, Jason passed away in 2019 due to complications from the second of two serious car accidents.

Every so often when he was still well, I would visit Jason at his home—because, you know, it's a nice thing to do to drop in on a guy in a wheelchair to make sure he's okay and not feeling forgotten. Even though I didn't make the 30-minute drive to his house very often, I really miss those visits. Over the years, I told myself I was going there because Jason probably needed me to call on him, but in reality I was the one who benefited from Jason visiting with me.

I always went when *I* needed a boost, under the guise that I would listen to how he was doing, even though I ended up talking the entire time, answering his questions about my work or what my kids were up to. I'd leave feeling like a really good person, that I had done something noble by taking my time to go see someone in need. But in truth, the reason I felt so good was because Jason made me feel good.

He lifted me up when I needed it on so many occasions, and that was because of his incredible outlook on life.

Jason believed that it was in his power to influence his outcomes. He really maintained that he could choose his response to any situation and that if he worked hard and was positive, he could transform any issue into something better than it was before. For Jason, life didn't just "happen" to him—although he found himself in some pretty devastating circumstances he had no control over. The first happened at age 15 when he became a quadriplegic after breaking his neck in a diving accident, and the second happened several years later when he was in his first life-threatening car accident. Jason believed that he had total control over his reaction to those happenings. His attitude had a profound effect on me and influenced my own outlook about my life, my family, and my business ventures.

Being around Jason helped me immensely. Likewise, I have found that it helps our organization when we look for people who have his same amazing attitude—especially when we go through dark periods of uncertainty and doubt. No matter how things unfold, good or bad, when we employ people who believe they can influence outcomes, our business just does better. These team players build everyone up over the long haul and help us see that we always get to choose how we respond to every situation. And that response can have a big impact on future events.

World-renowned psychologist and author Viktor Frankl is an expert on one's ability to choose, no matter the circumstances. As a prisoner of the Nazis during World War II, first in the Theresienstadt concentration camp—where his father perished—and later in Auschwitz—where his mother was killed—Frankl saw the best of human compassion and the worst of human depravity. He witnessed prisoners who, despite endless abuse and unspeakable torture, continued to show kindness to others. They might share a crust of bread or give a kind word. Frankl said, "They may have been few in number, but [these people] offer[ed] sufficient proof that everything can be taken from a man but one thing: the last of the human freedoms—to choose one's attitude in any given set of circumstances." From this it is obvious that in the face of difficulty, attitude is everything. And what's more, we are all free to choose our attitude, free to choose our reactions. We are free to choose who we will become and what we will work to accomplish.

British philosopher James Allen in his famed book on managing your own psychology, *As a Man Thinketh,* penned similar sentiment about the power we have to choose our outcomes: "Man is buffeted by circumstances so long as he believes himself to be the creature of outside conditions, but when he realizes he is a creative power . . . he then becomes the rightful master of himself."

When problems surface and progress seems to halt, as will be the case in every organization at various points along the way, the overall attitude the company possesses becomes the deciding factor in whether a business will succeed or fail—plain and simple. What's more, that organizational approach, while greatly influenced by the attitudes of owners and management at the top, is a collective product of the attitudes of the people you have chosen to put on your team, from general managers and supervisors to sales associates to technicians and service personnel. It turns out that a resilient attitude has more bearing on results than knowledge, work experience, education, or any other number of factors that businesses often try to throw at problems.

If the majority of your team has an attitude that reeks of helplessness, it's a pretty sure bet that the company will also be largely ineffective in turning trouble around (remember what happened to the 9th South store in the beginning when I hired unmotivated people just because they were cheap?). Conversely, if you have surrounded yourself with people who believe they have the power to control what happens to them, chances are your organization will be empowered as well.

I have acknowledged in several places throughout this book that my company's success and positive business culture cannot be attributed solely to my efforts. I think it's clear that the people you choose to work with are the key to growing a successful organization. I have learned that it is essential to hire individuals who are not only full of light (see chapter 1) and who are willing to build others up through their positive approach to work (chapters 2 and 3) but who can also *maintain* that positive energy and attitude in times when things don't look so good, whatever the cause and for however long.

Organizations that want to be successful (and maintain that success through the ups and downs) know the value of people who believe that they control their own outcome, who possess attitudes of hopefulness instead of helplessness, and who are not only filled with light and energy but who can keep that light burning brightly, regardless of the length or intensity of the challenges at hand.

In the following pages, I'd like to share with you examples of people who have influenced me with their resolute determination to affect outcomes for the better. I want to show that when business leaders and organization heads understand the power of the attitudes their team players possess and how those attitudes can either make or break their company, they will be very intent on hiring and retaining the people with the most determination, people who refuse to give up, and people who believe they can change the course of events in very remarkable ways.

Taking Control

When I began running the Big O Tires stores that Kory and I bought in 2006, I did so with a whole lot of dreams and very little practical experience. There were some dark days, as I have already admitted in earlier chapters. My mistakes were enormous. But I think that, because I have always taken responsibility for my mistakes and refused to play the victim, I was able to pull myself out of that gloom enough to see I needed other people with a can-do attitude to help get me out of the mess I had created. Such people believe that they control their outcomes—and are good at shunning fear. In our company today, we believe we control our destiny because we are in command of our attitude, desire, and effort.

My sister and former business partner, Kolette, is an amazing example of someone who takes control of her situation and believes that hard work and choosing her response to a situation can influence outcomes. During my short stint as a "fake" accountant at BFI Waste Systems where the kindhearted controller Annette gave of her time to teach me the principles of accounting, I also started up a wholesale distribution scrapbooking company with Kolette (who was married to Jason Hall), called Memories Complete. Kolette is a very talented artist and designer with a resilient attitude, and I learned many things about influencing my own situation from her approach to this business.

Even though Kolette and I pooled our resources, we still didn't have enough money for this venture, so while she and Jason were living with his parents in a suburb of New York City, Kolette asked a couple of wealthy families that she provided childcare for to loan us some seed money and they agreed. With their loans and the money a brother-in-law and our dad had loaned us, we had enough to get off to a small start.

As a gifted artist, Kolette designed a line of products, and it was my responsibility to get them to market. Our first attempt at selling products was at a trade show in Orlando, which would be attended by a few hundred retailers from around the country. We spent our entire startup fund on travel, a booth display, and the manufacture of enough product to sell to 100 retailers. We were banking on enough retailers liking our products that we could ship right away—and not on the alternative, which was that no one would like our merchandise and we would be forced out of business before we even got started! Fortunately, Kolette is the best, and our products were a big hit. We were awarded "Best New Company" at the trade show, and I had to call the manufacturer to order more merchandise.

Though we were very small, Memories Complete continued growing, and I used all of my vacation days at BFI to drive to trade shows where Kolette and I sold stickers and colorful, crafty papers. It was during one of these big events that Kolette overcame the forces of nature to take control of some unforeseen difficulties and ultimately influence her outcome.

We were at the nation's largest craft show in Chicago, and Jason was helping us show off our new product line. The time leading up to the show was always very stressful as Kolette prepared the launch of the new products. In addition to getting our merchandise ready, she was also designing a line of products for a larger manufacturing company, with which we had a new collaboration contract. This just added to the workload and the stress.

About halfway through the first day of the show, much of this stress seemed to affect Jason physically, and I noticed that his face had turned ghostly white. His lips were blue, and he was sweating. Kolette quickly left the show floor and rushed him to their hotel room to figure out what was wrong. Like the pro she is, she was able to assess his problems and get him stabilized without having to go to the hospital. When Jason's blood pressure returned to normal, she lifted him into bed and stayed by his side that afternoon to make sure he was recovering okay.

While Jason's health was the obvious priority, Kolette missed some key meetings with Walmart buyers and with purchasing agents of other large retailers, where she was supposed to be negotiating contracts to carry our products in their stores. While I could have handled the meetings, Kolette was the designer—the face of the company—and they wanted to meet with her, not me. I told the buyers she had an emergency and rescheduled for the next day.

Kolette stayed up most of the night with Jason, and she was absolutely exhausted the following morning at the trade show as we set up for the day. Now I was concerned not only about Jason's health but hers as well. I told her not to worry about the meetings, that we would do our best, and that she needed to rest. She said she would try to get some sleep and then left. At least that's what I thought.

An hour later, I went into the little two-foot space behind our display booth to get some supplies, and there, asleep on the cement floor, was Kolette. I woke her up and asked what she was doing; she said she didn't want to miss her meetings so she was just resting her eyes for a minute. I insisted that she go to the hotel, but she insisted that she go to her meetings (with concrete seam lines now etched into her face).

Kolette never once complained about Jason. She never once said any negative thing about having to care for him or being up all night. Like her husband, Kolette believes that she controls how she responds to difficult situations. When most people would have given up or tried to battle a different day, she believed that she could and would influence her outcomes on *that* day. She had her sights set on certain end results and was determined to see things through in that moment. And to her credit, she did, landing the contract with Walmart.

In his book *Learned Optimism*, professor of psychology and leading authority in the world on learned helplessness Dr. Marty Seligman explains that people like Kolette who believe they control outcomes and react with resiliency and strong personal capability have a different outlook on adversity than those who feel they have no control over anything. Dr. Seligman says, "Optimists recover from their momentary helplessness immediately. Very soon after failing, they pick themselves up, shrug, and start trying again. For them, defeat is a challenge, a mere setback on the road to inevitable victory . . . Pessimists wallow in defeat, which they see as permanent and pervasive." This powerful way of approaching difficulty is exactly what business leaders and organization heads need to keep their companies moving forward when forces seem to be pulling them back.

What to Look for in People Who Can Take Control

Here are some things I recommend assessing when you are seeking out team members who can truly take control when times get tough, as outlined by Dr. Seligman:

- They believe defeat is temporary.
- They do not see a set of problems as being pervasive; i.e., one particular problem does not affect everything else.
- They don't assume personal failure for the reason something bad happens; i.e., problems aren't necessarily all their fault. At the same time, they don't blame outside circumstances for every setback: They simply move forward without having to find a reason or cause for issues before tackling them.

"Such people," says Dr. Seligman, "are unfazed by defeat. Confronted by a bad situation, they perceive it as a challenge and try harder." He explains that those who take the opposite approach, who blame outside influences or their outcomes, have a different explanatory style than those with positive attitudes: "When explaining their misfortune [helpless people] will habitually say [things like], '. . . it's going to last forever, it's going to undermine everything I do.' Others, those who resist giving into misfortune say, '. . . it's going to go away quickly anyway, and besides, there's much more to life.'"

Because attitude is so important to the success of your organization, you may want to consider having potential hires complete questionnaires assessing how they would respond to both negative and positive situations. These types of assessments will help you see whether a potential hire believes in his or her own power to affect change, whether they are naturally more optimistic or look at the world in a helpless way, and how resilient they may be when faced with problems over time that come and go and can't necessarily be immediately resolved. Such assessments are available from many sources online and in Dr. Seligman's book *Learned Optimism*.

Shunning Attitudes of Helplessness

There will always be unforeseen problems that crop up in a business. I am continually amazed at all the many different ways things can go wrong; that's why in our stores, we have made it a priority to build teams composed of people who believe in themselves and can be hopeful about overcoming problems, who only suffer momentarily from defeat, and who are willing to try again—quickly. The speed at which these types of people can recover is key. While you may have some solid associates working for you who have fantastic attitudes and are filled with light and energy, if these same people can't bounce back swiftly when things go wrong, they may have a more helpless mentality and have not yet learned to take *full* control of a situation and turn it around. If you want to take your organization to the next level, it's important to find people who can bounce back quickly.

To illustrate what I mean, I'll use one of our strongest salespeople, Colton, as an example. He has been with our company for many years, and his quick wit keeps me on my toes. Customers love him because he is intelligent and thorough, rarely dropping the ball. He is also a good communicator.

In 2020, despite all his previous success, Colton experienced a rough year. His sales went down 34 percent from the prior year, while other salespeople at the same location had an increase in sales. When Miriam, my general manager, and I met with Colton to talk about his performance, he had no explanation. When asked what he thought he could do to improve, he responded that he was doing all he could.

His first reaction was typical for most of us: When a problem crops up, we will usually explain that we are doing our best. It's no fun to have to take responsibility. When things go badly, we don't want to admit we have any sort of control over the situation. It feels much safer to blame things on outside influences such as the economy, a pandemic, or any other number of forces at work in the world.

But then we showed Colton that the total number of cars the store had serviced was about the same as the prior year, and he was shocked to see that he had helped 1,200 fewer customers than the year before. To his credit, he realized quickly that this was actually something he could control. He resisted the urge to think such things as, "This is a big problem and it's probably going to affect my numbers for several months, nothing is going right, and I can't do anything about it." Instead, after being quiet for a moment, he said, "I'll fix it. This issue is over. It will no longer be a problem."

And he did fix it—immediately. The next day, Colton took back the control he had given up to the unknown cosmos and made the choice to help a lot more customers. He went back to providing his typical, outstanding service to all of those people. Instead of taking a helpless approach, Colton got hopeful again and took charge of something he had temporarily forgotten: He is in control and has the power to influence his own outcomes. Today Colton is better than

ever, and he has lifted up other teammates around him with his positive, can-do attitude.

Colton

Ways to Help Team Members Quickly Recover from a Setback

Having brightly lit, determined, happy people on your team who
have what it takes to turn things around quickly is always a smart
way to do business. But even the most optimistic people sometimes
need help staying hopeful. Following are some things you can do to
encourage your team to bounce back quickly from setbacks:

Take Control of Your Own Attitude First

According to a 2015 article in *Harvard Business Review*, "Research
shows that a leader's feelings are far more contagious than a team

member's so, while 'you don't want to suppress your emotions, you don't want to get stuck in a moody, negative space either,' says Susan David, a founder of the Harvard/McLean Institute of Coaching. Do whatever you need to move on from the disappointment so that you're ready to help your team deal with theirs. And don't try to fake it." The article goes on to explain, "You need to be genuinely in control of your feelings or your team will see through you."

Help People See Clearly Where the Problem Lies

You don't need to be a jerk when you point out problems, but be firm and don't sugarcoat anything either. With Colton, Miriam and I showed him the numbers, which clearly demonstrated what the problem was, and made it obvious to him what he had to do to fix it. State the facts such as, "You helped a lower share of customers this month," or, "Numbers are down from last month, let's look at why." You can be forthright when you focus on the facts, which helps you keep people motivated.

In addition to these tips, the *Harvard Business Review* article also recommends taking the following measures to help cultivate an attitude of hopefulness and more quickly turn things around when they aren't going as expected:

- **Shift the mood.** Talking facts and looking at the problem should only last so long. Don't get stuck commiserating. "Push your team to more open-minded thinking and discussion on how you will avoid similar mistakes in the future."

- **Tell a story.** Share a time when you made similar mistakes "It can be very powerful when a leader authentically shares a time when they had a crucible-type failure that became a stepping stone," says Sharon David, as quoted in the article.

- **Encourage collaboration.** Have a conversation about the lessons learned and what can be done in the future to avoid similar mistakes.

Staying Power

In chapter 1, I highlighted some pretty amazing people I am privileged to work with. They are outstanding because they are people with light. But this isn't the only reason. In addition to this positive, illuminating energy, they also have the ability to keep that light burning brightly for long, sustained periods of time, even when it is hard to do. This sustainable energy is important because it keeps team members involved and engaged during periods when the natural inclination might be to withdraw and retreat. To take an organization to a higher level, you will need to find (and retain) people who have this kind of staying power, who thrive on challenges, and who love to see things through to a successful conclusion.

Returning to Marty Seligman's research presented in *Learned Optimism*, I want to share the powerful observations he has made about people who have this unique staying power and who refuse to give up when faced with failure. Dr. Seligman presents the Princeton-Penn Longitudinal Study, conducted by Carol Dweck, wherein fourth grade schoolchildren "were divided into 'helpless' and 'mastery-oriented' groups. She then gave them a series of failures—unsolvable problems—followed by successes—solvable problems," Dr. Seligman explains. "Before the [unsolvable problems] were given there was no difference between the two groups. But once they started to fail an astonishing difference emerged. The children's problem-solving strategies in the 'helpless' [group] deteriorated down to the first grade level. They began to hate the task and talk about how good they were at [other things.] When the 'mastery-oriented' kids failed [at solving the problems] however, they stayed at their fourth grade level in their strategies, and while acknowledging they must be making mistakes, stayed involved. One mastery-oriented child actually rolled up her sleeves and said, 'I love a challenge.' They all expressed confidence that they would soon be back on track and they kept at it."

This kind of tenacity is what every organization needs in order to keep the ball rolling when times get tough or while experiencing a slump or downturn. Employees with such bulldog determination are able to remain involved and even enthusiastically engage in problem-solving, which can greatly influence not only what happens in the present moment but what will happen down the road.

When problems occur, no leader wants to work in a vacuum, trying to figure out solutions without the benefit of the entire team. If you haven't hired people you can turn to in a crisis, who aren't afraid of failure and who like the challenge of figuring out how to fix things because they believe they control their outcomes, your options for overcoming obstacles become very limited. People with light who aren't afraid to shine that light on difficult situations—even relishing the chance to crush the threat—have immeasurable value.

Examples in Business of People with Staying Power

You no doubt know Steve Jobs as a pioneer of the personal computer revolution in the 1970s and 1980s who became wildly successful as the founder of the Apple tech empire. But did you know he experienced his greatest failure *after* this long period of success? It was only because of his incredible perseverance that he was able to rise, like a phoenix, from the ashes and jumpstart his career again.

At just 20 years old, Jobs launched the small start-up computer company he named Apple—partly because he liked the fruit—with his friend Steve Wozniak in his parents' garage. Within ten years, Apple had grown into a $2 billion enterprise. But in 1986, when Steve was 30, Apple's board of directors fired him from the company he had created when they decided to take the organization in a different direction.

Jobs later said that getting fired from Apple was the best thing that ever happened to him because it gave him the freedom to think more creatively. He didn't see his defeat as a problem at all; like other great people with positive energy who believe in themselves and the innate power they have to influence outcomes, Jobs went on to found NeXT—a software company—in the 1990s and ultimately the animated motion picture production giant, Pixar. Because Jobs didn't see his ousting from Apple as a permanent and pervasive problem, he managed to maintain his positive energy and determination. He eventually landed himself back at Apple where, before his untimely death in 2011, he helped launch many of Apple's current line of immensely popular products.

Of course, the quintessential story of someone who believes they have the power to influence outcomes, no matter how long it takes, will always be of the great Thomas Edison and his work to invent the nickel-iron battery, the incandescent light bulb, and other inventions.

When Edison was a child, his parents took him out of school because teachers had labeled him "stupid" and "unteachable." Today, he would no doubt have been recognized as a kid with superior intellect—a child prodigy of sorts—but back in the mid-1800s, no one knew what to do with him.

As a teenager, he worked various odd jobs, ultimately getting fired from all of them. But nothing could stop him. He went on to become one of the greatest inventors of all time and a successful business leader. Over the course of his career, he filed 1,093 patents, many for inventions that would be groundbreaking, such as the phonograph, movie camera, and light bulb. But most of his inventions would be largely unsuccessful. This never seemed to faze him, even after a functioning nickel-iron battery eluded him, over and over again. At one point in the process, after five months of work and when none of Edison's ideas had panned out, his assistant wrote, "'Isn't it a shame that with the tremendous amount of work you have done you haven't been able to get any results?' Edison turned on me like a flash, and with a smile replied: 'Results! Why, man, I have gotten a lot of results! I know several thousand things that won't work.'" Now that's a person with light, and not only light but one that never seems to burn out! Edison did eventually master the nickel-iron battery and it was adopted in numerous railroad, forklift, and standby power applications throughout the twentieth century. It is this kind of tenacity, drive, and determination that ultimately wins the day.

While I will never claim to have anywhere near Edison's staying power in the face of adversity, I feel like I possess a portion of it, and I believe firmly that every organization that wants to succeed needs business leaders who also have a part of it and that see the value in finding team players who possess a portion of it as well. When you hire people with light and they can maintain that luminosity, even when things seem bad, your company will not only survive the slumps and setbacks, but it will eventually be great.

Operating with a team full of people who believe they are in control of what happens to them and who manage to maintain their positive energy over the long haul allowed us to set a new sales record in 2020 at our 9th South store with revenue of $8,442,439, making us the number-one store nationwide in the Big O Tires chain. With the chaos and confusion 2020 brought to the world, I believe we would not have been able to reach this kind of revenue without the determined, positive people I work with.

In conclusion, I want to leave you with this powerful quote by the great Dale Carnegie: "Most of the important things in the world have been accomplished by people who have kept on trying when there seemed to be no hope at all."

Conclusion

Trust the Process

"Success is never final and failure never fatal.
It's courage that counts."
—George F. Tilton

Our Big O Tires business has come a long way since the rough start we got off to in 2008. I wish I could go back and reassure my old self in that elevator at the convention in Dallas that things would get better. But life just does not work that way. There is a process to learning. It has to be like that. But humans hate uncertainty, so of course we think it would be so great if we could just know all would be well in the end. *If only I knew it would all work out, I could relax a little bit and enjoy the ride so much more.* At least that's what I used to tell myself.

But that is a lie.

The only way to learn and progress is to go through the process, both the good and bad, the ups and downs, the hard times and the inexplicably joyous moments. The only way to get better, smarter, nimbler, wiser, and more patient, is to make decisions and see how they play out. There is no crystal ball. If it weren't that way, there would be no tension, no wondering, no hoping, no faith, and no improvement. It has to be a challenge or we learn nothing. We must go through this process or we make no progress.

For me, the most beneficial progress I have made by trusting in the process and being willing to go through it rather than around it or away from it, is learning and appreciating—very deeply—that it's all about people. People are what matter most. Each person has individual gifts and talents, and each person has flaws and imperfections. There are no perfect people to hire, and there are no perfect customers to sell to.

Naturally there are times when working with people tries my patience. Sometimes they make my head hurt, and sometimes they make me want to sell my company and go back to that cubicle at BFI Waste Systems, where as an accountant I had to relate to nothing but numbers. And the people I work with sometimes tell me I try their patience in the same way as well.

But finding great people, teaching and training people, and learning to trust and love people—both those you work with on your team and those you service who walk through your doors—is what makes the process fun; it's what makes the journey interesting and exciting. Seeing someone progress and sharing success with other people is what makes the risk of business ownership worthwhile. It can be a messy process with a lot of ups and downs, but I am learning to trust that process. I hope you can, too.

In 2021, we started the year at the 9th South store with a goal of reaching $8,700,000 in sales. A few months into the year, Miriam Cordova and I suggested to the team a goal of $9,000,000, but they balked at that, thinking it was too much (with everything going on in the world and such; you know, that sort of thinking . . .).

Fine.

But by the end of March, sales were up enough that the team made the decision that they would indeed try to reach that $9,000,000 mark. By the end of July, they thought they could hit $9,500,000, and by mid-December they blew through $10,000,000, a feat considered impossible by many professionals in our industry. Our team now believes that even this record will be shattered . . . very soon.

Notes

Introduction

Jack London, "To Build a Fire," *The Youth's Companion* (May 29, 1902). "The most beautiful stories always start with wreckage."

Robert A. Whitman, "Building A Winning Culture: A Top Priority for Leaders," (2019). "Nearly everything about your organization—including your strategy, products, and systems—can be replaced, except one thing: the effectiveness of your people. Culture is the ultimate competitive advantage." Retrieved from https://www.franklincovey.com/content/dam/fcdc/downloads/culture-whitepapers/FC_WinCul_TopPri_WhitePaper.pdf.

Malcolm Forbes, *Forbes*, "Too many people overvalue what they are not, and undervalue what they are." Retrieved from https://www.forbes.com/quotes/6399.

Chapter 1

Patricia Hruby Powell, *Lift as You Climb: The Story of Ella Baker* (New York: Simon and Schuster, 2020), quoting Ella Baker: "Give light, and people will find the way."

Leslie Allen and Amy Bouque, "Do It Right: Attract and Keep the Best People," *Automotive News* (August 12, 2019). "Because [customers] can find the same deals . . . in just a few clicks on the internet, your employees are critical to winning over new customers—and keeping them."

Oliver Wendall Holmes, *The Poet at the Breakfast Table* (New York: Houghton, Mifflin & Company, 1883), p. 294. "It is the province of knowledge to speak, and it is the privilege of wisdom to listen."

Og Mandino, "Take the attitude of a student, never be too big to ask questions, never know too much to learn something new."

The 14th Dalai Lama, "The key to happiness is peace of mind. This is not something that can be bought. Inner peace has to be cultivated by each of us from within." Retrieved from https://www.dalailama.com/messages/transcripts-and-interviews/the-purpose-of-life-is-to-be-happy.

Allen and Bouque, *Automotive News* (August 12, 2019). "Recruiting [the right people] starts at the top. You have to have the right culture . . . to entice the right people to join your team. [You must build a culture] with a lot of intention, about how you speak to each other, how employees work with customers, how they talk about other departments."

Howard Schultz, *Pour Your Heart Into It: How Starbucks Built a Company One Cup at a Time* (New York: Hyperion, 1997), p. 81. "Whatever your culture, your values, your guiding principles, you have to take steps to inculcate them into the organization early in its life so that they can guide every decision, every hire, every strategic objective you set."

Allen and Bouque, *Automotive News* (August 12, 2019). "Fleming Ford, vice president of people analytics at ESI Trends, a Florida consulting firm . . . underscores the importance of top leaders in attracting and keeping good workers. 'General managers have to get better at the people part—explaining the vision, inspiring the team,' she says. 'They've got to get over the idea that they're selling cars [or tires or automotive repair, or whatever else]; their job is to manage the people who sell [these things].' Ford suggests a daily huddle with managers reinforcing different core values."

Mark Wetterau, Chairman and CEO of Golden State Foods, 2020.

Chapter 2

Gordon B. Hinckley, "You can't build a great building on a weak foundation. You must have a solid foundation if you're going to have a superstructure." Retrieved from https://www.pbs.org/wgbh/americanexperience/features/mormons-hinckley/.

Potentialife.com, "The Pygmalion Effect," (November 2017). "A series of studies has demonstrated that leaders and authority figures play a major role in the successes or failures of the people under their supervision."

Ibid., "Harvard professor J. Sterling Livingston replicated [the Rosenthal/Jacobson] findings in the workplace. Managers were told that their employees had been given a test to identify potential and were then given the names of those who had done best. But as in the Rosenthal experiment, the names had been chosen randomly. In his write-up of the study . . . Livingston noted that . . . manager's expectation had a huge impact on the performance and career progress of their employees."

Ibid., "'The single most reliable indicator of how successful an employee will be, is the extent to which somebody believes in [them].'"

Charles Dickens, *A Christmas Carol* (New York City: Hodder and Stoughton, 1911), p. 15. "Think of people below you as if they were really fellow passengers to the grave, and not another race of creatures bound on other journeys."

Anne Shiess, *Got Kids . . . Now What?* (Idaho Falls, Idaho: Anne Shiess, 2021). "Believing in your children, really believing in them, will compensate for the many mistakes you will make with them."

Eric Ries, *The Lean Startup* (London: Penguin Group, 2011), p. 236. "Remember, most mistakes are caused by flawed systems, not bad people."

Chapter 3

Charles L. Allen, "Remember that you are needed. There is at least one important work to be done that will not be done unless you do it." Retrieved from https://artsandculture.google.com/entity/charles-l-allen/m07ttp2?hl=en.

Warren Buffet, "Price is what you pay; value is what you get" in a letter to Berkshire Hathaway shareholders, 2008.

Denny Warnick, executive vice president and chief operating officer of In-N-Out Burger, as quoted to the author: "Harry and Esther Snyder founded In-N-Out Burger in 1948 upon the strong values of . . . providing the very friendliest service to your customers. From the beginning, the Snyders treated associates like family, realizing that we're only able to meet our high standards with exceptional [people], who are dedicated to making that happen. Paying higher wages is one important way to make our associates feel great about working at In-N-Out. It's helpful in creating an upbeat and customer-focused atmosphere, with relatively low turnover, which leads to more experienced teams working our restaurants."

Chapter 4

Dan Montano, "Lions or Gazelles?" *Economist Newspaper Ltd.* (July 6, 1985), p. 37. "Every morning in Africa, a gazelle wakes up. It knows it must run faster than the fastest lion or it will be killed. Every morning a lion wakes up. It knows it must outrun the slowest gazelle, or it will starve to death. It doesn't matter whether you are a lion or a gazelle—when the sun comes up, you'd better be running."

Edward Perlman, "His Eye Is on the Rails," *New York Times* (July 3, 1958), p. 15. "After you've done a thing the same way for two years, look it over carefully. After five years, look at it with suspicion. And after ten years, throw it away and start all over."

Craig Manning, *The Fearless Mind* (Springville, Utah: Cedar Fort, Inc. 2009), p. 36. "We have to be constantly reaching for more."

Ibid., "[Even though] the most successful [person] on the team at one time was the weakest (Patrick was not the biggest physically), he had the greatest weapon anyone could have: his mind was fearless."

Alex Hutchinson, *Endure: Mind, Body, and the Curiously Elastic Limits of Human Performance* (New York: HarperCollins, 2018), p. 10. "What's crucial is the need to override what your instincts are telling you to do (slow down, back off, give up). . . . Endurance implies something more sustained: holding your finger in the flame long enough to feel the heat."

Rodolfo Costa, *Advice My Parents Gave Me: and Other Lessons I Learned from My Mistakes* (Lima, Peru: Rodolfo Costa, 2009). "Cultivate an optimistic mind, use your imagination, always consider alternatives, and dare to believe that you can make possible what others think is impossible."

Chapter 5

Jens Wolff, "The way you do small things is the way to do all things." Retrieved from https://www.goodreads.com.

Annette Franz, "11 Simple Ways to Make Customers Feel Valued," *Forbes* (February 24, 2020). "Putting the 'customer' in the *customer experience* means that you're thinking about the humans in front of you, listening to them, understanding them, designing the experience for them. And it's a reminder that without customers, you have no business."

Mariah Raner, "Why Customer Trust Is Important for Business Growth" (March 2021). "When companies build trust, they enable customers . . . to advocate their business. These customer evangelists [help] increase brand visibility and attract more customers. Building trust establishes a stronger customer base, gives you a competitive edge, and cultivates continued growth." Retrieved from Brandcraft.com.

Laurie McIntosh, "You are serving a customer, not a life sentence. Learn how to enjoy your work," retrieved from http://blog.hubspot.com.

Robin Blakely, "11 Simple Ways to Make Customers Feel Valued," *Forbes* (February 24, 2020). "Actively listening to people does more than earn trust—it earns loyalty and even love for who you are and what you do. So, listen. Make sure you hear properly. Ask relevant questions."

iEduNote.com, "How to Value Your Customers," (2021). "Shoving a questionnaire down [customer or vendor] throats pre-emptively is a bit heavy-handed, but if you have a place customers can easily access to leave feedback and how their experience was, that will pay off. You'll receive direct feedback from your customers, and they'll end up getting a more satisfying experience if you implement some fixes for them."

Annette Franz, "11 Simple Ways to Make Customers Feel Valued," *Forbes* (February 24, 2020). "Show them you are acting on their feedback. Tell them, 'We hear you and we're doing something about it.' When you ask customers for feedback, let them know that it was received, that you heard what they are saying and that you're going to do something with it."

iEduNote.com (2021). "The entire process, from perusing your products to finalizing payment should be as smooth and enjoyable as possible, with clear indications of how much you'll charge and how to proceed at each step. If you manage to make buying things from you fun and easy, you've struck gold."

Mark Savinson, "11 Simple Ways to Make Customers Feel Valued," *Forbes* (February 24, 2020). "Clients may not like the truth, they may not have the budget or resources to tackle the whole truth, but telling the truth enables you to work with them to make the best decisions and find the best outcomes based on their resources and priorities."

iEduNote.com. (2021). "Business transactions can easily become impersonal, so extending even the smallest amount of courtesy by treating your customer like a distinct human being instead of a dollar sign pays dividends. Any small detail counts, so long as it demonstrates you astutely paid attention to every detail about them that you could . . . make it personal."

D. J. Sebastian, *The Selling Revolution* (Miami, Florida: Samuelson Publishing, 2019).

Andrew Carnegie, "Carnegie On How To Get Rich," *St. Louis Globe-Democrat* (October 15, 1899), section 3, column 4. "No man will make a great business who wants to do it all himself, or to get all the credit of doing it. That spirit is fatal, and the sure proof of a small mind."

Carl W. Buehner, *Richard Evans' Quote Book* (Salt Lake City: Publishers Press, 1971), p. 244. "I've learned that people will forget what you said, people will forget what you did, but people will never forget how you made them feel."

Betsy Sanders, *Fabled Service* (San Diego: Pfeiffer & Company, 1995), p. 15. Service, in short, is not what you do, but who you are. It's a way of living that you need to bring to everything you do if you're to bring it to your customer interactions."

Chapter 6

James Allen, *As a Man Thinketh* (New York City: St. Martin's Press, 2019), p. 25. "Good thoughts and actions can never produce bad results; bad thoughts and actions can never produce good results. This is but saying that nothing can come from corn, but corn, and nothing from nettles but nettles."

Victor Frankl, (Boston: Beacon Press, 1959), p. 66. "They may have been few in number, but [these people] offer[ed] sufficient proof that everything can be taken from a man but one thing: the last of the human freedoms—to choose one's attitude in any given set of circumstances."

James Allen, *As a Man Thinketh*, p. 15. "Man is buffeted by circumstances so long as he believes himself to be the creature of outside conditions, but when he realizes he is a creative power . . . he then becomes the rightful master of himself."

Martin Seligman, *Learned Optimism* (New York City: Simon & Schuster, 1990), p. 142. "Optimists recover from their momentary helplessness immediately. Very soon after failing, they pick themselves up, shrug, and start trying again. For them, defeat is a challenge, a mere setback on the road to inevitable victory. . . . Pessimists wallow in defeat, which they see as permanent and pervasive."

Ibid., p. 142. "Such people are unfazed by defeat. Confronted by a bad situation, they perceive it as a challenge and try harder. When explaining their misfortune [helpless people] will habitually say [things like], '. . . it's going to last forever, it's going to undermine everything I do.' Others, those who resist giving into misfortune say, '. . . it's going to go away quickly anyway, and besides, there's much more to life.'"

Amy Gallo, "How to Help Your Team Bounce Back from Failure," *Harvard Business Review* (February 27, 2015). "Research shows that a leader's feelings are far more contagious than a team member's so, while 'you don't want to suppress your emotions, you don't want to get stuck in a moody, negative space either,' says Susan David, a founder of the Harvard/McLean Institute

of Coaching. Do whatever you need to move on from the disappointment so that you're ready to help your team deal with theirs.
And don't try to fake it. You need to be genuinely in control of
your feelings or your team will see through you."

Ibid. "Push your team to more open-minded thinking and discussion on how you will avoid similar mistakes in the future."

Ibid. "It can be very powerful when a leader authentically shares
a time when they have a crucible-type failure that became a stepping stone."

Martin Seligman, *Learned Optimism.* "Children were divided into
'helpless' and 'mastery-oriented' groups. She then gave them a
series of failures—unsolvable problems—followed by successes—
solvable problems. Before the [unsolvable problems] were given
there was no difference between the two groups. But once they
started to fail an astonishing difference emerged. The children's
problem-solving strategies in the 'helpless' [group] deteriorated down to the first grade level. They began to hate the task
and talk about how good they were at [other things.] When the
'mastery-oriented' kids failed [at solving the problems] however,
they stayed at their fourth grade level in their strategies, and while
acknowledging they must be making mistakes, stayed involved.
One mastery-oriented child actually rolled up her sleeves and
said, 'I love a challenge.' They all expressed confidence that they
would soon be back on track and they kept at it."

Steve Jobs, from his 2005 commencement address, Stanford
University.

Thomas Edison, *Edison: His Life and Inventions,* 2 (New York
City: Harper & Bros., 1910), p. 615–16. "'Isn't it a shame that with

the tremendous amount of work you have done you haven't been able to get any results?' Edison turned on me like a flash, and with a smile replied: 'Results! Why, man, I have gotten a lot of results! I know several thousand things that won't work.'"

Dale Carnegie, "Being Discouraged Never Pays," *The Marshall News Messenger* (January 29, 1942), p. 6, column 5. "Most of the important things in the world have been accomplished by people who have kept on trying when there seemed to be no hope at all."

Conclusion

George F. Tilton, "Thoughts On the Business of Life," *Forbes* (November 1, 1948), p. 34, column 3. "Success is never final and failure never fatal. It's courage that counts."

Please visit www.kentcoleman.com. You can sign up for my newsletter and find links to my social media, @TireGuyKent, if you are interested. I love to hear from my readers. If you want to share your story, ask questions, or book me to speak, please contact me via my website, above.

Thank You

Thanks so much for taking the time to read *It's Not About the Mangos*. I'd be so grateful if you'd take a few minutes to leave a review wherever fine books are sold, as reviews are the lifeblood of an author.

About the Author

As a young kid, Kent Coleman had no aspirations of owning a tire store. He wasn't fascinated with anything automotive; in fact, he found that world rather boring. While other kids were playing with action figures, Kent was figuring out how to make money parking cars, selling chocolate bars, or any number of other things he did in his attempts to make a few extra bucks. Other boys wanted to be a baseball player or a firefighter, but Kent dreamed of being a "business man," exhibiting his entrepreneurial spirit from a young age and launching several enterprising ventures throughout his youth.

In college, Kent realized he wanted to know more about the ins and outs of business and earned an MBA from Utah State University in 2002. He then launched over a dozen successful companies and today owns a chain of auto repair franchises and various commercial properties. Even though he is no "car guy" himself, his auto repair shops are consistently some of the highest-producing stores in the nation. His strength lies in getting to the root of an issue quickly, his knack for asking the right questions to solve the right problems, and of course the way he values the people who have helped him succeed in business.

Along with his love of building organizations with a strong, people-oriented culture, Kent enjoys sharing his business experience as a speaker, writer, and die-hard entrepreneur. He also loves spending time with his family in the mountains, at the beach, and on the slick rock of the Mountain West. He lives in Utah with his wife, Crystal, and their four children.